LINES

OF CONTENTION

ALSO BY J. G. LEWIN AND P. J. HUFF

How to Feed an Army

How to Tell a Secret

Witness to the Civil War (ed)

Collins
An Imprint of HarperCollins Publishers

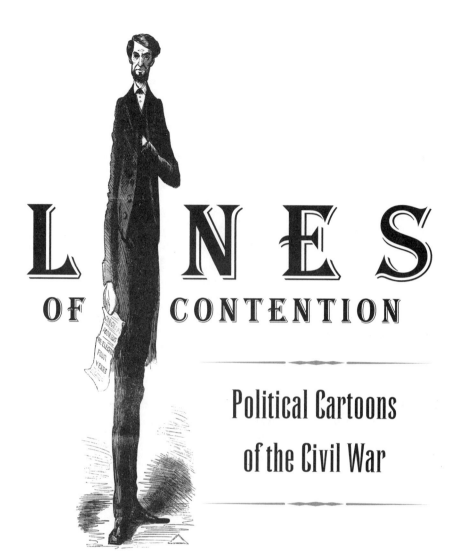

L NES

OF CONTENTION

Political Cartoons
of the Civil War

J. G. LEWIN

AND

P. J. HUFF

HarperCollins books may be purchased for educational, business, or sales promotional use. For information, please write: Special Markets Department, HarperCollins Publishers, 10 East 53rd Street, New York, NY 10022.

FIRST EDITION

Designed by Ralph Fowler / rlf design

Library of Congress Cataloging-in-Publication Data
　　Lewin, J. G.
　　　Lines of contention : political cartoons of the Civil War / J. G. Lewin
　　and P. J. Huff. — 1st ed.
　　　　p.　cm.
　　　Includes bibliographical references and index.
　　　ISBN 978-0-06-113788-4
　　　1. United States—History—Civil War, 1861–1865—Caricatures and
　　cartoons.　2. United States—Politics and government—1861–1865—Caricatures
　　and cartoons.　3. United States—Politics and government—1849–1877—Caricatures and
　　cartoons.　4. Political culture—United States—History—19th century.　5. American wit
　　and humor, Pictorial.　I. Huff, P. J.　II. Title.
　　　E647.L55 2007
　　　741.5'973—dc22　　　　　　　　　　　　　　　　　　　　　　2007017605

07 08 09 10 11　ID/QW　10 9 8 7 6 5 4 3 2 1

Contents

Introduction

This book is not, strictly speaking, a military history of the Civil War. Only tangentially does it deal with the movements of great armies, of strategies and tactics, of battles and leaders and specific incidents of that most horrific period in American history.

Rather, *Lines of Contention: Political Cartoons of the Civil War* explores popular views of the war, and incidents surrounding the war, as they were presented by the editorial cartoonists of the day. As such, it becomes a history of the incidents, attitudes, and politics of the war as seen through the eyes of contemporary commentators. The cartoonists tried to put events, issues, and people in proper perspective. They attempted to enlighten, to reflect, and, perhaps at times, to persuade public opinion. The cartoonists' job was to encapsulate a situation into a few panels. By definition they were forced to oversimplify their topic. But in so doing, they often cut to the nub of the matter and presented it in terms that were easily understood. Humor in all its forms—irony, puns, satire, parody—was employed in trying to get the point across.

It is difficult for twenty-first-century readers to grapple with these issues as they did. From our perspective, nearly 150 years after the fact, we like to think that we are aware of the issues and how they were eventually resolved. But if we can approach these cartoons without preconceived beliefs, we can begin to understand the mindset, the confusion, and the resolve of the people who lived through these traumatic events.

Since the creation and publication of cartoons was a commercial enterprise, it follows that the themes employed and the messages conveyed carried a certain resonance with the audience. A publisher wasn't going to spend good money to produce a product that no one wanted to buy, and no one would buy a product that espoused a position significantly at odds with their own—particularly since that product would ridicule the purchaser's opinion.

So the study of these cartoons, even in a cursory way, does provide insight into the attitudes of the audience. This was the mass communication of the day. The humor is broad and not necessarily overly sophisticated. Reflected here are the prejudices of the day, and often that is far from what our contemporary society would consider either appropriate or in good taste. But that is precisely the point of this book: these cartoons weren't drawn for *us;* they were drawn for *them*. They were commentary on the times. If we can immerse ourselves in that commentary, we begin to immerse ourselves in those times.

Perhaps it is too much of a stretch, but the ideal would be a thought experiment in which we place ourselves into the front parlors and barrooms of nineteenth-century America and eavesdrop on the conversations taking place there. Obviously we cannot physically travel back in time, but we can take a mental journey. And in lieu of actually listening in, we can read these cartoons and take part in the conversation.

The cartoonist's art was relatively new at the time. Although the first attempt at a graphic representation of an editorial opinion (the term *cartoon* hadn't yet been coined) had been published more than a century before, in 1754 by Benjamin Franklin, use of the medium was not commonplace.

John Leech, artist on the staff of *Punch* magazine in London, can rightly claim to have originated the art form. In July 1843 the weekly humor magazine published Leech's parody on their government's competition to decorate the new houses of Parliament. The drawing showed walls heavily bedecked with fine art while the population of

"Join, or Die." May 9, 1754. *Pennsylvania Gazette.* Benjamin Franklin is credited with publishing the first cartoon in the colonies with this image of a severed snake. The cartoon was used to illustrate Franklin's editorial stance against a "disunited state" of affairs in the colonies. The debate was whether to unite the militias under a single command during the conflict that became known as the French and Indian War.

London starved. At the time, the rough sketch submitted by an artist to a patron as a proposal for the finished piece was known as a cartoon. Leech transformed the term by calling his drawing a cartoon, and history was made.

At roughly the same time, a new kind of newspaper, an illustrated newspaper, was slowly making its appearance on the scene. Printing technology of the day did not lend itself to imagery. Producing the images was both time-consuming and costly, since the original piece of art had to be, first, simplified to a series of lines (as opposed to continuous tones of gray) and then painstakingly etched onto blocks of wood that could be run through a printing press. Some daily newspapers experimented with the process in the early 1850s but quickly abandoned it because it was so costly and the space could be better employed by filling it with paid advertisements.

But what didn't necessarily work in a daily newspaper began to make economic sense for a weekly publication. The novelty alone would help to sell newspapers. So in some of the larger cities a weekly illustrated newspaper began to take hold.

The *Illustrated London News* was the first commercially viable example. *Punch* appeared shortly thereafter, but with the twist of changing its focus from news to commentary and humor. In the United States, several attempts had been made to emulate the *Illustrated London News* (including one by P. T. Barnum, always on the lookout for a novelty), but none met with success until the launch of *Frank Leslie's Illustrated Newspaper* in 1855. *Harper's Weekly* began publishing in 1857, and *Vanity Fair* (an American version of *Punch*) first appeared later that same year.

With the illustrated newspapers came the editorial cartoons. Cartoons became one of the more popular features of the papers and began to flourish with two, sometimes four, published in each edition. And the creators came to be in demand. With deeper pockets, *Harper's Weekly* would lure the best reporters, field artists, and cartoonists to its staff.

The journalistic standards employed in the mid-nineteenth century were significantly different from those employed in the early twenty-first century in that the political leanings and commentary were not confined to the editorial pages. Most newspapers were strongly allied with a political party, and this bias colored the reporting of news events. The cartoonists followed, and often amplified, that bias. At the same time, the cartoonists were breaking new ground as they explored notions of caricature, symbolism, and allegory.

The general popularity of the political cartoon was not limited to the newspapers, however. A number of private publishers began to issue political commentary in the form of broadsides and lithographic prints. The names of some of the publishing houses have been lost, but we know these publications were issued in Philadelphia, Cincinnati, Chicago, Buffalo, and New York. Several of the publishers are still fairly well known—Currier & Ives and T. W. Strong, for example. Their output was broad-based and not limited to the politics of the day.

In addition to the broadsides, stationery containing cartoon commentary was published and sold. Typically the cartoon would appear in the upper left-hand corner of the envelope. It was often overtly and simply patriotic, such as an eagle or a flag. But nearly as often it contained a message in the form of a sarcastic representation of the issue of the day.

Copyright laws were far less stringent than today, and the three primary media—stationery, broadsides, and newspapers—would borrow liberally from one another. A different engraver's hand would be readily apparent, but the cartoon was essentially the same.

So the message was getting out to the public at large. Whether it was sarcastic, sardonic, or simply patriotic, cartoons would hammer home the essence of the topic at hand. And the popularity of a humorous, graphic representation of a serious issue grew. Publishers of broadsides and lithographs flourished. Illustrated newspapers became established as an independent genre. And citizenry on both sides of the Mason-Dixon Line accepted cartoons as an element of the discourse.

There was nothing funny about the Civil War. It was a time of terror. Of carnage. Of absolute brutality. Of uncertainties and imponderables. For a full appreciation of the times, the study of people and attitudes is at least as important as the study of armies. These cartoons can bring us one step closer to that appreciation.

LINES

OF CONTENTION

· 1 ·

THE IRREPRESSIBLE CONFLICT

The Divisive Issues Defined

T HE TRAGEDY that has come to be known as the
American Civil War did not just happen overnight. The stresses and central issues—primarily
the question of slavery's continued existence or total
eradication—had been the subject of continuous debate
and uneasy compromise since the original thirteen colonies had banded together to force political disunion with
Great Britain in 1775.

From the earliest days of the young Republic until
the middle years of the 1800s, the tone of these debates
became increasingly shrill, while the nature of these
compromises became increasingly tenuous. Those who
advocated extreme positions in the North called for the

immediate end to all slavery within the boundaries of the growing United States. Those who advocated extreme positions in the South called for unfettered extension of the practice throughout the new western states and, indeed, throughout the entire country. But the majority of the population—the white majority—stood in the middle ground. The politicians in Washington attempted to represent their constituencies. And as the political climate became increasingly polarized during the 1850s, those in the middle ground began to lean further and further toward the extremes, and the tensions increased.

Senator Seward saw it as an "irrepressible conflict." Soon the compromises would have to come to an end and a final determination would have to be made. The cartoonists attempted to illustrate the many facets of the primary issues in simple and uncluttered terms.

It is an irrepressible conflict between opposing and enduring forces, and it means that the United States must and will, sooner or later, become either entirely a slaveholding nation, or entirely a free-labor nation.

—U.S. senator William Henry Seward, October 1858

MR. JONES, pictured in this *Harper's Weekly* cartoon, is understandably confused. If the newspapers cannot agree on the facts of what is taking place, how is even the most informed reader to form an intelligent opinion on the events of the day?

If you were paying attention to the news, reading the papers, it was difficult to get the facts straight. Something about a fort somewhere in South Carolina. *Harper's Weekly* captured the confusion. If the daily papers couldn't get it straight, how was anyone to know what was really happening?

Slavery was an abomination, according to the abolitionists in the North. Preachers throughout New England, the Mid-Atlantic region, and the new western states railed against it and demanded that it end. So it ended in those states. But that wasn't enough for them. Slavery needed to be abolished everywhere and for all time.

Many in the South, on the other hand, believed slavery was necessary and good. It was, first of all, profitable.

The plantation system produced cash crops of cotton, tobacco, and sugarcane for markets in the North and in Europe. These crops, particularly cotton, were necessary as the raw materials that helped fuel the mills and factories of the Industrial Revolution. The Southern, slaveholding point of view also held that the slaves themselves needed guidance, discipline, and protection. They could not fend for themselves. It was a common belief that many slaves would starve if they were suddenly forced out on their own. In any case, slavery was a Southern institution, and Yankee abolitionists had no right to tell Southerners what to do.

At least, when you cut through all the smoke and rhetoric, that seemed to be the state of things. But there was an awful lot of smoke and rhetoric. Certainly rational men, moderate men, could find a middle ground.

It was beginning to look as if the hotheads in the North and in the South were heading in a bad direction, but it was hoped that cooler heads would prevail.

READS THE PAPERS.

Our Friend, Mr. Jones, who is deeply interested in the condition of the country, takes all the Papers, and reads them thoroughly. The following Dispatches puzzle him somewhat:

The Cabinet have issued the orders for the Evacuation of Fort Sumter.—*Herald.*

It is at last decided that Fort Sumter shall be reinforced.—*Times.*

Orders were sent off last evening to Reinforce Major Anderson at all costs.—*Tribune.*

It is believed that Major Anderson Evacuated Fort Sumter by order of the Government last evening.—*World.*

{ *Harper's Weekly*, April 13, 1861 }

"LIKE MEETS LIKE"

GARRISON--Well, my friend, at last we meet in unity to destroy 'this accursed union'.

KEITT--'Twas only a misunderstanding this many years. We were always one at heart.

{ Leslie's Illustrated, 1858 }

THE IRONY of the situation, according to *Leslie's Illustrated,* was that the most extreme of positions were actually advocating a single solution: disband the Union. That would certainly solve the problem of this "house divided against itself," as one of the western politicians termed the state of the nation in 1858.

William Lloyd Garrison (pictured at right) was an ultra-abolitionist. Based in Boston, his weekly newspaper, the *Liberator,* became the de facto voice of the movement to end slavery in the United States. While others in the movement called for the gradual emancipation of the slaves, as had been accomplished in New England during the early years of the nineteenth century, Garrison said that only the immediate and complete emancipation of slaves was acceptable. It was during one of his public speeches that a member of his audience pointed out that the Constitution protected slavery. If that was true, Garrison was purported to have said, then the Constitution should be burned.

Lawrence M. Keitt, a member of the House of Representatives from South Carolina, pictured at left, was just as absolutely rigid in his position as was Garrison in his. He was a firebrand calling for secession. The prevailing attitude in the North and the workings of the government in Washington could not be trusted, he said, to uphold the rights granted to the states by the Constitution. The only remedy, according to Keitt, was to leave the Union and assume sovereign status.

It was increasingly difficult to discern the difference between patriotism and treason. The moralist from the North advocated burning the Constitution while a congressman from the South advocated disbanding the Union.

A FORECAST of the Civil War may have been predicted most accurately and succinctly by London's *Punch* magazine in 1856. A Southern planter, rough-hewn and armed, stands facing a contemplative businessman from the North. Between the two, a slave tears apart a map of the United States, the rip seemingly to follow the Mason-Dixon Line (the boundary between Maryland and Pennsylvania, a geographic, if not political, dividing line between North and South).

The caption's pun was intentional. The country was being torn apart by the business of slavery—the buying and selling of people, and the profits that were produced by slave labor. The South and the North raged over the righteousness of their relative positions, while those at the center—the black slaves—did not participate in the debate.

THE UNITED STATES—A BLACK BUSINESS

{Punch, November 8, 1856 }

ACCORDING TO this cartoon in *Harper's Weekly*, the strength of the United States lay in the unity that binds individual states into one cohesive unit. *E Pluribus Unum*—one out of many. George Washington is the "Old Man," and the quarreling sons are the individual states. As he reprimands his rebellious offspring, his foot rests upon a fasces.

The fasces, as a symbol, dates to ancient Rome. It is a bundle of sticks, originally birch rods, bound tightly together, with a red ribbon, around a central ax. As the caption here maintains, the fasces is a symbol of strength in unity.

Further, a fasces is the symbol of strong central authority. And it was exactly a strong federal authority that the South chose to leave. The Southern states were no longer thinking of a strong, centralized Union; they were, instead, thinking more along the lines of a confederacy.

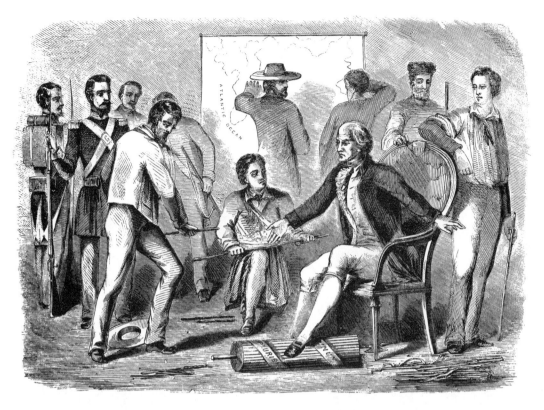

THE OLD MAN AND HIS SONS

An old Man had many Sons, who were often quarreling with one another. When the father had exerted his authority, and used other means to reconcile them, but all to no purpose, he at least had recourse to this expedient: he ordered his Sons to be called before him, and a short bundle of sticks to be brought; then he commanded them each to try if, with all his might and strength, he could break it. They all tried but to no purpose; for the sticks being closely and compactly bound up together, it was impossible for the force of man to do it.

After this, the father ordered the bundle to be untied, and gave a single stick to each of his Sons, at the same time bidding him try to break it, which when each did with all imaginable ease, the father addressed them to this effect: "O, my Sons, behold the power of unity: for if you, in like manner, would but keep yourselves strictly conjoined in the bonds of friendship, it would not be in the power of any mortal to hurt you; but when once the ties of brotherly affection are dissolved, how soon you become exposed to every injurious hand that assaults you!"

MORAL: UNION IS STRENGTH

{ *Harper's Weekly*, February 2, 1861 }

MISS COLUMBIA CALLS HER UNRULY SCHOOL TO ORDER

{ Leslie's Illustrated, January 7, 1860 }

MISS COLUMBIA appears to be annoyed with the students in her class. The lesson she has prepared is on the Constitution. The book is sitting on her desk, and many of her students already have it open and are giving it close study. The Mason-Dixon Line runs right through the middle of the classroom.

There is a disruption right in front of the desk. Horace Greeley, publisher of the *New York Tribune* and ardent abolitionist, appears to be hurrying back to his side of the room and may have stumbled over the Mason-Dixon Line. Below Greeley, another seems to have tripped. This is William Seward, senator from New York. Upon his slate is written "Irrepressible Conflict," a reference to a speech he made on the Senate floor wherein he predicted that secession would lead to an irrepressible conflict in the land. At the time this cartoon was published, Seward was considered the front-runner for the nomination of the fledgling Republican Party.

In the background, under the planters' hats, a student scrawls, "Let us alone," on the wall of the classroom. When the general movement for secession was under way, this was the plea of the Southern states. They hoped to leave in peace. But peace does not appear to reign in the classroom.

It is noteworthy that absent from the scene is James Buchanan, president of the United States.

Left: James Buchanan (1791–1868). The fifteenth president of the United States, elected to office in 1856. Despite the power of his position as chief executive and commander in chief, he did nothing to stop, or even delay, seven states from seceding from the Union and commandeering federal property (including munitions and fortifications), thus setting the country on the path to the Civil War. Most biographies of Buchanan note that the majority of historians rank him among the worst, if not *the* worst, of all who have held the office of president of the United States.

THE RAREY SYSTEM was a fairly new procedure, in vogue in 1861, for training horses. South Carolina, pictured here as the frisky colt, did not want to be brought under control, and certainly not under the control of President Buchanan.

James Buchanan of Pennsylvania was elected to the office of president on the Democrat ticket of 1856, defeating former president Millard Fillmore, who ran as the American Party (Know-Nothing) candidate, and John C. Frémont, the first candidate of the Republican Party. Although he had had a long and distinguished career in the House of Representatives and the Senate and as a diplomat, Buchanan was an attractive candidate primarily because he had been out of the country, serving as minister to Great Britain, during the preceding years of divisiveness. But his skills on Capitol Hill and as a diplomat failed him, and the country, now.

Buchanan was a Northern politician with decidedly Southern inclinations. He tried to walk a fine line between the two camps and, as a result, satisfied neither side. Although he opposed secession, he did nothing to stop it. In fact, several members of his cabinet aided the process by shifting resources (particularly munitions and war matériel) to Southern arsenals, where they might be seized by rebel states.

NEW APPLICATION OF THE RAREY SYSTEM

Mr. Rarey Buchanan doesn't see why he can't put the Federal stays on that spunky little colt Miss South Carolina. When he tried to pat her—she bites; when he tried to apply the strap—she kicks. He really doesn't see what is to be done with her—s'poses she'll have to have her own way. To which remark Miss Carolina doesn't say, neigh!

{ *Leslie's Illustrated,* January 26, 1861 }

Doctor North to Patient South—Help you! Of course! We will first with your assistance, take off your legs & then fix you up nicely on these Constitutional Amendments.

South—Can't see it.

{ Unattributed Southern broadside, 1861 }

THIS BROADSIDE appeared on the streets of the South as commentary. A patient with a broken arm seeks healing from a doctor. Congress here takes on the persona of "Doctor North" (he may be Thaddeus Stevens, the abolitionist congressman from Pennsylvania). The doctor, eyeing his patient with a broken arm, proposes to amputate the patient's legs and offers a wooden limb (labeled "Constitutional Amendment"). "Patient South" doesn't think this is going to help.

The course of action being proposed by the North was not only unacceptable to the South, it was also close to absurd, according to this broadside. Congress was attempting to work through the crisis by debating fresh legislation and constitutional amendments. But the South would accept nothing less than absolute guarantees that it would be free from any Northern interference. This was much more than the North was willing to concede.

THE PALMETTO TREE is native to South Carolina and was quickly adopted as the symbol of secession. It appeared on flags, on cockades, and, as pictured here, on a patriotic envelope (earlier in this chapter, it appeared as a pattern on the pantaloons of Lawrence M. Keitt).

Secession was in the air. Southern states called it independence.

Unionists—that is, those in the North who were committed to the preservation of the Union—were starting to call it treason. The penalty for treason was death by hanging. According to this envelope, that would be the outcome of South Carolina's secession.

THE FRUIT OF THE PALMETTO TREE-SON

{ Patriotic envelope, 1861 }

COLUMBIA AWAKE AT LAST.

{ *Harper's Weekly,* June 8, 1861 }

FAIR COLUMBIA was finally awaking to the idea that some of the states were actually going to try to leave the Union; eleven had already adopted resolutions of secession.

Holding the Constitution and again invoking the spirit of George Washington (pictured in the background), Columbia appears aroused. She is far more substantial than are the Southern states. They appear rather scrawny in their planter's caps and their pantaloons emblazoned with "secession" and "treason." But they are armed. They have torn the Constitution and are attempting to steal away, but Columbia has decided to hold them.

Neither side believed the other would actually carry through its threats. The North didn't think the South would really leave the Union; it was all bluff and bluster in an attempt to get its own way. The Southern states didn't think the North would try to stop them from leaving; secession would be accomplished without bloodshed and the two regions of the country could go their own way in peace.

THE SOUTH was in trouble, and about to get even more of it, according to this patriotic envelope. It had fallen off a safe and stable dock, one that had the glory of the American eagle with its military might, provisions, and the recognition of foreign nations. From this dock, it was about to flounder in an unfriendly sea, one that included the monster of secession. All would be lost if it did not cling to "this 'ere Flag" of the Union.

Patriotic envelopes such as this were popular in the North throughout the war.

I say old fellow, just hold on to this 'ere flag, or YOU ARE LOST.

{ *Patriotic envelope, circa 1861* }

South Carolina, having declared its independence from the Union, had decided that it wanted no foreign military presence. What this meant in practical terms was that it intended to confiscate all federal property within its borders. The state's militia had already moved upon and had seized federal arsenals and their contents in Charleston. They now wanted Fort Sumter, which sat in the middle of Charleston's harbor and commanded all approaches from the sea.

Governor Francis Pickens, in his new capacity as a head of state, had informed President Buchanan through a diplomatic delegation that he would not tolerate the reinforcement or resupply of the garrison. He asked politely when he could expect to see the garrison withdrawn. Buchanan wavered.

Currier & Ives depicted the situation with the governor threatening force, about to light a "peacemaker." But, according to the printmaker, the big gun was pointed in the wrong direction. Even so, Buchanan is shown throwing up his hands and pleading for time. Soon there would be a new president, and South Carolina would no longer be Buchanan's problem.

SOUTH CAROLINA'S 'ULTIMATUM'

{ *Currier & Ives, 1861* }

Vanity Fair, in this cartoon, shows Columbia (the North) praising Major Robert Anderson while a sheepish President Buchanan (complete with the palmetto flag of South Carolina in his hair) merely sits and frets.

Major Anderson, commanding the garrison in Charleston, believed his position was untenable. He and his men were living in Fort Moultrie, on the harbor shore. The earthworks that faced the city were low, since no one had anticipated danger approaching from that direction. So low, in fact, were the walls that the entire fort could be seen, and fired upon, from the second-story windows of the houses across the street. A much safer position was available to him in the form of the unfinished and unmanned Fort Sumter in the middle of the harbor. Anderson repeatedly requested permission to move his command to Sumter.

President Buchanan, in the meantime, had given assurances to Governor Pickens of South Carolina that no hostile moves would be coming from Anderson's command. That included garrisoning Fort Sumter. So Anderson's repeated requests were ignored.

But Anderson could wait no longer. Secession was a fact. The federal arsenal in Charleston, including all its weapons and artillery, had been seized by the South Carolina militia. Anderson's men were in danger.

So under the cover of darkness on the evening of December 26, 1860— six days after South Carolina adopted its ordinance of secession—Anderson moved his command to Fort Sumter. And there were screams of protest throughout the land. South Carolinians said they felt threatened by the garrison's presence in the harbor. The state's delegation to Washington believed they had been lied to. And even in Buchanan's cabinet there were calls for Anderson's removal.

A GOOD BOY

Columbia: "Never mind, Bobby Anderson, if your father doesn't like what you have done, I do."

{ *Vanity Fair*, January 12, 1861 }

OUR NATIONAL BIRD AS IT APPEARED WHEN
HANDED TO JAMES BUCHANAN. MARCH 4.1857

THE IDENTICAL BIRD AS IT APPEARED A.D. 1861.
I was murdered i'the Capitol
Shakespere

{ *Strong's Dime Caricatures,* 1861 }

J AMES BUCHANAN'S tenure in office as the fifteenth president of the United States was coming to a close, and no one, it seemed, welcomed it more than did Buchanan himself.

In early 1861, after Lincoln's election but prior to his inauguration, Strong's Dime Caricatures, a publisher of broadsides, distributed this commentary on the health of the country. The country was, according to this broadside, apparently sound and in fine feather when Buchanan took office, but some four years later it had lost one leg to secession and was hobbled in the other by anarchy. It is little wonder that the national emblem looks worn and tired.

· 2 ·

THE PRESIDENTIAL QUICKSTEP

The Election of 1860

THE ELECTION OF 1860, in the view of many historians, was the most important election in the history of the United States. Four major candidates stood for the presidency. Of these, three—the Southern Democrats' John C. Breckinridge, the Northern Democrats' Stephen A. Douglas, and the Constitutional Unionists' John Bell—were viewed as voices of compromise. Only one, the Republicans' Abraham Lincoln, was generally viewed as an agent of change. It made little difference to the electorate what the candidates themselves said. Each candidate was judged by the statements and promises of his party and his supporters.

The Democrats could not agree on a unified direction for their party, nor on a single candidate to lead all factions. The party split into Northern and Southern wings, each with its own platform and each with its own candidate. The Constitutional Union Party, composed primarily of the remnants of the old Whig Party, fielded a candidate who was the only one to be listed on the ballot in every state, but had little other claim to prominence. And a growing fear was that whoever was left, the Republican candidate would win almost by default.

Throughout the South, plans were being made against the possibility of a Republican in the White House. Should such a disaster occur, many in the South were prepared to leave the Union rather than live under a Republican president. And there was ample justification for James Buchanan's belief that he was to be the last president of a wholly United States.

AS THE SEASON of political conventions approached, it was clear that few wanted another four years of the Buchanan administration.

Appearing in *Vanity Fair* in early April 1860, just two weeks prior to the Democrats' convention in Charleston, South Carolina, this cartoon shows the president as an Irish house servant answering to his employers. He is clutching his bag, labeled "Wheatland" (the name of his estate in Lancaster, Pennsylvania), while Mrs. Columbia, as the voice of the North, tells him the news, ". . . we sha'n't want your services after next March."

Mrs. Columbia appears to be at her sewing, repairing a map of the United States that has been torn apart along the Mason-Dixon Line. The gentleman behind her is not identified, but from his relaxed and familiar posture we are to infer that he is the man of the house. This is an early representation of Uncle Sam (although he had yet to be given that name).

So this is the American house, with Mrs. Columbia and her consort as masters. On the wall is a Shield of Liberty (Mrs. Columbia wears the same as an earring), and a bust of Washington looks on from the shelf. "Biddy" Buchanan, caretaker of this house, is being fired.

Buchanan had originally wished to run for a second term. But it soon became obvious, even to him, that his wishes meant little to the rest of the country.

SOON TO BE OUT OF A JOB

Mrs. Columbia: "Well, Bridget, I guess we sha'n't want your services after next March."

Biddy Buchanan: "An' shure thin will yezz be afther giving me back me charackther?'

{ *Vanity Fair,* April 7, 1860 }

LITTLE STEPHEN A. TRYING TO CLIMB INTO A VERY HIGH CHAIR.

{ *Vanity Fair*, April 14, 1860 }

SENATOR Stephen A. Douglas of Illinois, the "Little Giant," was the front-runner for the Democrats' nomination going into the 1860 convention. But it was not at all clear that he would get the nod.

The "very high chair," of course, was the presidency. And that entitled him, among other things, to have the "pap" of political appointments. But he was attempting to climb into the presidency on the backs of slaves and a very shaky stool that was Kansas.

Douglas was the principal sponsor of the Kansas-Nebraska Act of 1854. The act called for voters of individual states to determine whether their state would allow or ban slavery. The idea of letting those directly involved determine the issue was called "popular sovereignty" by its supporters; detractors lampooned it as "squatter sovereignty."

As Kansas prepared to vote prior to its admission to the Union, the state was flooded with settlers. Both sides of the question sponsored families to move to the territory, and neither side chose to express its opinions solely through the ballot box. Kansas erupted into a battleground, with killings and atrocities on both sides. It came to be known as "Bleeding Kansas." Douglas, rightly or wrongly, took much of the blame.

And in 1860, should he be the nominee of the Democratic Party, he would carry this legacy with him to the voters.

THIS GAME of nominating a candidate was played with very high stakes. Both men, the Democrat on the left and the Republican on the right, were very serious players.

The Democrats deadlocked in their convention, and they could not decide on a nominee. Hampered by his record on Kansas, and viewed as being anti-slavery, Douglas could not gather the votes of enough delegates to secure his nomination. The South would not support him. The North would not support anyone else. The Democrats adjourned without naming a candidate. They would meet again in June, in Baltimore this time, to determine their nominee.

The Republican Party had yet to meet. Their convention was scheduled to take place in late May in Chicago. The scheduling had been deliberate. Republicans wanted to see whom they would be against in the November elections. But it was not to be so.

In this cartoon published immediately after the Democrats adjourned, *Vanity Fair* pictured it as a high-stakes game of poker. It appeared now that the Republican would be forced to show his hand first.

THE POLITICAL GAME OF BLUFF

{ Vanity Fair, May 12, 1860 }

A "RAIL" WESTERN GENTLEMAN

{ *Leslie's Illustrated,* July 1860 }

ABRAHAM LINCOLN. Lincoln the rail-splitter. Lincoln of the West. Lincoln, the tall and ungainly; the disheveled. Lincoln the surprise.

It was widely believed that either William H. Seward, senator from New York, or Salmon P. Chase of Ohio would receive the Republicans' nomination for president. Both were able, honest, and ambitious politicians. But both had enemies. And while they were busy attempting to garner support as the primary choice of delegates, neither had focused on being the second choice of delegations already committed to "favorite son" candidates. Lincoln, however, did. So when the convention could not come to a decision between Seward and Chase, the delegates turned to their second choices, and there stood Lincoln.

Lincoln was certainly not unknown. Earlier in the year, he had made a speaking tour of New England and New York and had drawn large audiences to hear his views on the issues of the day, particularly slavery. By all accounts, his audiences had been impressed by his speeches. In 1856 his name had been mentioned as a candidate for vice president on the ticket with John C. Frémont. Still, he was a dark-horse candidate in 1860. A significant factor in his gaining the nomination was the simple fact that no one really objected to this western lawyer, who was presented as a man of the people, a man who had split rails and worked as a common man rather than as a professional politician.

Vanity Fair looked to Shakespeare for inspiration to illuminate the state of affairs brought on by disunity among the Democrats. In *A Midsummer Night's Dream,* the two lovers, Pyramus and Thisbe, are forced to speak to one another through a wall. The cartoon sees Buchanan as the wall itself. And Douglas cannot see the bliss of the nomination of a united party.

When the Democrats reconvened in Baltimore in mid-June 1860, they were a party deeply divided over slavery. John C. Breckinridge of Kentucky, the sitting vice president (pictured at left), was the choice of the proslavery faction, while Stephen A. Douglas of Illinois (pictured at right) was a voice of the presumed middle ground. Between the two stood Buchanan, nominal head of the party.

Buchanan gave his support to his vice president, Breckinridge, but it made little difference. When it appeared certain that Douglas would get the nomination, delegates from the Southern states walked out of the convention. Reassembling in Richmond within the week, the Southern Democrats held their own convention and nominated Breckinridge.

The party split. Rather than the unity of a single party, it would present voters with two distinct tickets in the general election in November. Each party would field its own nominee for the presidency—Douglas for the Northern faction, Breckinridge for the Southern.

THE MODERN PYRAMUS AND THISBE

Thisbe by John C. Breckinridge. *The Wall* by James Buchanan. *Pyramus* by Stephen A. Douglas.
Pyramus speaks: "O, wicked Wall, through whom I see no bliss!"—"A Midsummer-Night's Dream,"
Act V, Scene 1.

⟨ Vanity Fair, July 1860 ⟩

THE SPLIT-TAIL DEMOCRACY

The deed is done, their day is o'er,
Two possums fought at Baltimore;
Now let them scratch, now let them wail,
Old Abr'm has them "in a rail."

{ Rail Splitter, July 21, 1860 }

T HE REPUBLICANS published a weekly newspaper, dubbed the *Rail Splitter,* during the campaign. Each issue would contain a cartoon and frankly biased examination of the positions of the various candidates. The cartoon here appeared shortly after the twin Democratic conventions announced their candidates.

The rhyme is a little forced, but the message is clear: the Democrats could not agree on a message or a single candidate during their Baltimore convention, so the Republican rail-splitter would take them on and defeat them individually.

Lincoln's reputation as a rail-splitter dated from his days in rural Illinois when he would work all manner of jobs to sustain himself. A campaign biography told of his first job after he had struck out on his own. Lacking a suit of clothing, he "split four hundred rails for every yard of brown jeans dyed with white-walnut bark that would be necessary to make him a pair of trousers." His image as a simple, perhaps rough-hewn man of the people was cultivated by his party during the election.

A FOURTH CANDIDATE entered the race when the Constitutional Union Party nominated John Bell. This was the last attempt of the old Whig Party to play a role in national politics. Theirs was a platform of self-proclaimed moderation. They stood for healing the nation and pulling the states back together. They did not say, however, exactly how this was to be accomplished.

So this broadside, printed in Cincinnati, pictures Bell (at far right) with a pot of glue poised to begin repairs while the three other candidates do their best to rip the map of the United States to pieces.

Lincoln and Douglas, pictured at far left, are fighting over the northern and western states while Breckinridge takes the South.

To some extent, this was an accurate representation, but only to a degree.

Although there were four major national candidates, only three ran in the North (Lincoln, Douglas, and Bell) and only three ran in the South (Breckinridge, Douglas, and Bell). Lincoln's name did not even appear on the ballot in nine Southern states.

It really was a race between Lincoln and Douglas in the North and between Douglas and Breckinridge in the South. Bell played the role of spoiler, pulling votes from all candidates.

The results appeared lopsided (see chart below).

Lincoln carried every free state, except New Jersey. Breckinridge carried eleven slave states, while Bell took Virginia and the border states of Kentucky and Tennessee. Douglas captured only New Jersey and Missouri.

Lincoln was now president-elect, and the stage was set.

	Popular Vote		*Electoral College Vote*
	COUNT	PERCENTAGE	
Lincoln	1,865,908	39.8%	180
Douglas	1,380,202	29.5%	12
Breckinridge	848,019	18.1%	72
Bell	590,901	12.6%	39

DIVIDING THE NATIONAL MAP

{ Broadside, Fall 1860 }

Top to bottom:

John Bell (1797–1869). Candidate for president of the Constitutional Union Party during the election of 1860. Although initially opposed to secession, he changed his allegiance when Tennessee joined the Confederacy.

John C. Breckinridge (1821–1875). Candidate for president of the Southern Democratic Party during the election of 1860. Although Kentucky stayed in the Union, Breckinridge went south, joining the Confederate army and rising to the rank of major general. He was appointed secretary of war by Jefferson Davis and served in that capacity until the fall of the Confederacy.

Stephen A. Douglas (1813–1861). Candidate for president of the Northern Democratic Party during the election of 1860. A staunch believer in democracy, he was the champion of "popular sovereignty," which dictated that local populations should decide the issue of slavery.

Abraham Lincoln (1809–1865). The sixteenth president of the United States, first elected to the office in 1860. The North considered him a moderate; the South considered him a rabid abolitionist.

This is the way the
North received it

This is the way the
South received it

PRESIDENT LINCOLN'S INAUGURAL

{ *New York Illustrated News,* March 9, 1861 }

THIS IS THE FIRST published political cartoon of Thomas Nast, an artist who would be credited as the greatest cartoonist of his age, and it reflects the opposing perspectives of the North and the South.

Lincoln was hailed throughout the North as a man of reason who would stand on sound legal principle. He would keep peace throughout the land and, as the cartoon shows, weigh equally the claims of the North and of the South. Lincoln, indeed, is pictured in the role of Blind Justice with a crown of laurel leaves.

The South didn't see him quite the same way. He was the oppressor, the uncompromising abolitionist. He was elected to make war and to subjugate the South.

It may be that both views were at least partially correct.

SOUTH CAROLINA did not see the need to wait until Lincoln's inauguration in March 1861 in order to take action.

The artist pictures the South, complete with planter's hat, whip, and gun, in a sullen state of mind. In the text accompanying this cartoon, the editors of *Punch* noted that South Carolina, "in an ecstasy of slave-owners' rage," had ordered that all copies of the Scriptures be burned. "Moreover," it continued, "she calls a convention and declares that she is going to separate from the Union, and be an independent State, and have representatives at the courts of Europe."

South Carolina did, indeed, secede. Just four days after the general election, her legislature authorized a convention to explore the question. That convention adopted the ordinance of secession on December 20, 1860. Over the course of the next six weeks, the states of Mississippi, Florida, Alabama, Georgia, Louisiana, and Texas (in that order) followed suit. All had left the Union prior to Lincoln's inauguration. Delegations from these states met in Montgomery, Alabama, and formed the provisional government of the Confederate States of America in early February

{ *Punch*, December 1, 1860 }

1861, naming Jefferson Davis of Mississippi as its president.

Thus, before Lincoln had even taken office, the Confederacy was organizing itself into a distinct country.

One of the ironies of the situation was that the two sections of the country, polarized and diametrically opposed to one another, chose moderates to lead them. Lincoln, who was to lead the North, believed that, barring a constitutional amendment, the federal government did not have the power to abolish slavery. Davis, a slave owner who was cool to the idea of secession, was to lead the South.

THIS PATRIOTIC envelope ridiculed the notion of an independent confederacy of states. Jefferson Davis, the provisional president of this new government, would learn that soon enough.

The North was not prepared to let the Southern states go. It believed in a union of all the states for all time under the rule of the Constitution. And it was prepared to fight to maintain this Union.

THE FLAG
OF
A NEW CONFEDERACY.

{ *Patriotic envelope, 1861* }

It was, in fact, a constitutional question. And some constitutional scholars maintain that the Southern states may have been within their rights to withdraw from the original Union. The Constitution itself is silent on the question, and scholars point to the Tenth Amendment to the Constitution, an element of the original Bill of Rights, as justification for their position. It reads:

> *The powers not delegated to the United States by the Constitution, nor prohibited by it to the States, are reserved to the States respectively, or to the people.*

This is the so-called states' rights amendment. Some scholars point to this and argue that if secession is not expressly prohibited by the Constitution (and it is not), then it may have been unconstitutional for the federal government to prohibit it.

Unconstitutional or not, the federal government was about to prohibit it.

I N THIS CARTOON, Lincoln is pictured as a workman with a pot of
glue whose job it is to pull the two
pieces together. In addition, as president, he would be responsible for putting together a cabinet of advisers.

Although seven states had legally and
irrevocably (in their view) withdrawn
from the Union by the time this cartoon
was published, there was still hope in
the North that Lincoln could somehow
repair the damage.

This is an early cartoon of Lincoln.
The artist apparently hadn't yet received
word that the president-elect had
started to let his beard grow in the new
style of the times.

A JOB FOR THE NEW CABINET MAKER.

{ *Leslie's Illustrated*, February 2, 1861 }

OLD ABE—" *Oh, it's all well enough to say, that I must support the dignity of my high office by Force—but it's darned uncomfortable sitting—I can tell yer.*"

{ *Leslie's Illustrated*, March 2, 1861 }

LINCOLN was coming to Washington amid a growing clamor for war; it was as if he were being carried by military events. Southern states were seceding from the Union; Northern states were demanding their return. And, like sitting atop bayonets, it could not have been comfortable.

Lincoln had transformed his trip from Springfield, Illinois, to Washington, D.C., into a grand tour. Over a period of two weeks, he stopped in cities along the way to participate in a variety of formal ceremonies, to address legislatures, and to be feted by local dignitaries. All the while, the news of developments within the burgeoning Confederacy was dogging his steps.

A government had been formed in Montgomery, complete with a constitution, a legislature, and a president. "All we ask is to be let alone," said Jefferson Davis to the new Confederate Congress.

That did not seem to be an option for President-elect Lincoln, who saw his primary responsibility as the preservation of the Union.

LINCOLN HAD BARELY taken office when criticism of his actions became regular fodder for the Democratic press. This cartoon, published just a few days after his first inauguration, pokes fun at Lincoln's actions during a crisis.

The newspaper report, quoted in the captions of the four panels, is essentially correct. Lincoln's last stop before Washington was to have been in Baltimore. But Allan Pinkerton's detectives, then in the employ of the railroads, had uncovered a plot to assassinate the president-elect. It was Pinkerton who came to Lincoln, then in Harrisburg, Pennsylvania, to warn him of the plot and to suggest an alternative means of travel.

Whether or not he attended ceremonies, Lincoln would need to change trains in Baltimore. Pinkerton had arranged for Lincoln to travel on an earlier train, incognito but not in disguise. He had also arranged to cut communications so advance word of Lincoln's new plans would not fall into the hands of the Baltimore conspirators.

When Lincoln was presented with the plan, he resisted because he thought it would make him appear foolish and frightened. But against his better judgment he relented and placed himself in Pinkerton's hands. Traveling with just two close friends, Lincoln arrived in Washington one day early, unannounced and without ceremony. When he called upon President Buchanan, as depicted in Panel 4, he is shown as frightened and uncertain (two common complaints often leveled at Buchanan).

The newspapers loved it. They did not believe that a conspiracy existed (it did). They claimed that Lincoln traveled in disguise (he didn't). They claimed that he fled in the night to pass safely through Baltimore (this was a little close to the mark).

The incident overshadowed his two-week tour and the inauguration. Lincoln always regretted his decision.

(1.) THE ALARM.

"On Thursday night, after he had retired, Mr. LINCOLN was aroused, and informed that a stranger desired to see him on a matter of life and death. * * * A conversation elicited the fact that an organized body of men had determined that Mr. LINCOLN should never leave the City of Baltimore alive. * * * Statesmen laid the plan, Bankers indorsed it, and Adventurers were to carry it into effect."

(2.) THE COUNCIL.

"Mr. LINCOLN did not want to yield, and his friends cried with indignation. But they insisted, and he left."

(3.) THE SPECIAL TRAIN.

"He wore a Scotch plaid Cap and a very long Military Cloak, so that he was entirely unrecognizable."

(4.) THE OLD COMPLAINT.

"Mr. LINCOLN, accompanied by Mr. SEWARD, paid his respects to President BUCHANAN, spending a few minutes in general conversation."

THE FLIGHT OF ABRAHAM

(As Reported by a Modern Daily Paper)

(1.) THE ALARM. "On Thursday night, after he had retired, Mr. LINCOLN was aroused, and informed that a stranger desired to see him on a matter of life and death. * * * A conversation elicited the fact that an organized body of men had determined that Mr. LINCOLN should never leave the City of Baltimore alive. * * * Statesmen laid the plan, Bankers endorsed it, and Adventurers were to carry it into effect. (2.) THE COUNCIL. "Mr. LINCOLN did not want to yield, and his friends cried with indignation. But they insisted, and he left." (3.) THE SPECIAL TRAIN. "He wore a Scotch plaid Cap and a very long Military Cloak, so that he was entirely unrecognizable." (4.) THE OLD COMPLAINT. "Mr. LINCOLN, accompanied by Mr. SEWARD, paid his respects to President BUCHANAN, spending a few minutes in general conversation."

{ *Harper's Weekly*, March 9, 1861 }

OUR GREAT ICEBERG MELTING AWAY

{ Harper's Weekly, March 9, 1861 *}*

BUT THERE WAS HOPE, according to *Harper's Weekly*. A new sun was on the horizon with the inauguration of this new president. James Buchanan, the iceberg, was going away.

"If you are as happy, my dear sir, on entering this house as I am leaving it and returning home, you are the happiest man in this country" were Buchanan's parting words to the new president.

THIS CARTOON, published as a broadside immediately following Lincoln's inauguration, portrays Lincoln, as schoolmaster, in a position of authority over erring schoolboys.

A group of schoolboys has decided to play a little hooky, skipping their classes for a skinny-dip in the pool of secession. Some are already in the pool, while others are in various states of getting ready to jump in. But when Lincoln approaches, the fun is over and all make ready to come back, like good boys, to school. All, that is, except one.

South Carolina, with the palmetto flag on the ground beneath her, is in Lincoln's grasp. She is biting him on the hand while shouting defiance.

But the significance is that Lincoln is in charge.

That the federal government was in a position of authority over the individual states was a new concept. Up to this point, the states were in charge, and the federal government acted as coordinator rather than as leader. Things were changing with Lincoln.

Novelist and historian Shelby Foote correctly observed that prior to the Civil War, it was perfectly acceptable to say, "The United States are . . . ," but that after the war the correct form was to become "The United States is. . . . " The term *United States* was to change in usage from plural to singular. That, too, may have been subtle, but the transformation in attitude was to have profound impact upon the way this society began to define itself.

THE SCHOOLMASTER ABROAD AT LAST

"Come, boys! They are all waiting for you—you have staid there long enough! I will forgive you this time if you will try to do better in the future. Only think what a bad example you show the other boys!" (Lincoln)

"Boys, he is after us! I reckon I'll reconsider!" (Schoolboy #1)

"Well, we've been playing hooky long enough; I guess I'll go back!" (Schoolboy #2)

"If that's UNCLE "ABE," I'll put my trowsers right straight on again." (Schoolboy #3)

"You let me alone! I will play in the mud if I like!" (South Carolina)

{ Strong's Dime Caricatures, March 1861 }

· 3 ·

AND THE WAR CAME

The Conduct of the War

BY THE TIME Abraham Lincoln took the oath of
office as the sixteenth president of the United
States, the Confederate States of America had
already seated a distinct House of Representatives, a Senate, and an executive (complete with cabinet), had written
and ratified a constitution, and had even conducted a national contest for the design of a new flag. In fact, the
"Stars and Bars," the first national flag of the Confederacy, was formally dedicated and raised in Montgomery,
Alabama, on the very day that Lincoln took his oath of
office.

The Confederate States of America, in other words, was an established fact when Lincoln began his presidency.

Many throughout the Confederacy expected the North to just let them go. There was an expectation that while the North would wail and protest, it would take no steps to stop the South from leaving the Union. More experienced heads, however, knew war was inevitable. And both sides began to mobilize. But neither side was prepared for the long and bloody struggle that was to come.

Both parties deprecated war, but one of them would make war rather than let the nation survive, and the other would accept war rather than let it perish, and the war came.

—Abraham Lincoln, second inaugural address

PRIOR TO the start of real hostilities, the Southern states attempted to exercise their autonomy from their former government by appropriating Federal property and facilities within their borders. Forts, arsenals, customhouses, lighthouses, naval yards, and all their contents were seized by militias and dedicated to use by the Confederacy.

According to this cartoon, the South, in the form of Jefferson Davis, is a thief in the night. When confronted by an aroused Uncle Sam, he pleads to be left alone as he runs away loaded down with Federal property.

Just as Lincoln had become a symbol of the Federal government in Washington, so Jefferson Davis, newly elected president of the Confederate States of America, had come to be a symbol of Southern secession.

Unlike Lincoln, however, Davis did not have the gift of flowing rhetoric; his memorable statements are few. Perhaps the most enduring words came during his first message to the Confederate Congress in March 1861 when he said, "All we ask is to be let alone." The artist quotes Davis here.

———————

Left: Jefferson Davis (1808–1889). President of the Confederate States of America. As an administrator, he was prone to delving into the minutest details and was loath to delegate authority, but even his harshest critics conceded that he was wholly devoted to the new nation and the Confederate government.

UNCLE SAM. "Hallo there, you Rascal! Where are you going with my Property, eh?"

JEFF. DAVIS. "Oh, dear Uncle! ALL I WANT IS TO BE LET ALONE!"

{ *Harper's Weekly*, June 1, 1861 }

THE UNION had a bulldog in Winfield Scott, "Old Fuss and Feathers," commanding general of the army. In this cartoon, Scott is the bulldog fronting the might of the North. Munitions, supplies, and financial resources back him as he taunts the Southern greyhound wearing a collar labeled "Jeff." Indicating a juicy bone labeled "Washington Prize Beef," Scott asks, "Why don't you take it?" as Davis skulks off, tail between his legs, back to his lonely bale of cotton. The South had cotton, but not much else, and didn't have the strength to wrest the bone from the Union's bulldog.

It is not too much of an exaggeration to say that no one had a greater impact on the American military during the first century of the Republic than did Scott. He first rose to prominence during the War of 1812 when, posted to Buffalo, New York, he led an invasion of Canada. During the Mexican War, he commanded the invasion of Mexico, and a series of brilliant campaigns there led to the capture of Mexico City. Winfield Scott was considered to be one of the greatest military minds ever produced by the United States.

But at the outbreak of the war, he was seventy-five years old and had been in

WHY DON'T YOU TAKE IT?

{ *Currier & Ives, July 1861* }

the service for more than fifty years. Renowned as a connoisseur, he was simply too old and too fat to even mount a horse. Still, he was the commander of all Federal armies and widely viewed as a hero. Although he was a native of Virginia, there was no question where his sympathies lay at the outbreak of war.

One irony of this cartoon is that Washington probably could have been taken if the Confederacy had mounted an attack. There were few Federal troops in the city (Scott himself made his headquarters in New York). The volunteer militia of the District was decidedly pro-Southern. Washington, center of the Federal government and symbol of the Union, was vulnerable.

Alexander H. Stephens, vice president of the Confederate States of America, first raised the cry "On to Washington!" shortly after the attack on Fort Sumter, and plans were afoot within the Confederacy to capture the city. It wasn't until Massachusetts and Pennsylvania rushed volunteer units to defend the capital in late April 1861 that Washington became an armed camp and was made safe from capture.

———

Left: Winfield Scott (1786–1866). Scott had the distinction of serving as a general officer longer than any other man in U.S. history. He was called "Old Fuss and Feathers" for his pomp and adherence to regulations (and as an uncomplimentary comparison to "Old Rough and Ready" Zachary Taylor). Scott eventually resigned his commission in November 1861 after having served as a general officer for forty-seven years. Scott retired to West Point, New York, where he died in 1866.

NEITHER SIDE expected hostilities to last longer than six months, and both, of course, expected their side to prevail. The popular view in the North was that the Confederacy would fold almost immediately after the first battle.

This comic broadside, published in Philadelphia late in 1861, portrays the South, in the person of Jefferson Davis, as full of bluster and martial certitude as he heads off to war. But flip it over, and a totally different picture emerges: Davis as a donkey; Davis as simply foolish.

Jeff. Davis going to War.

AN

Jeff. returning from War.

Entered, according to Act of Congress, in the year 1861, by E. Rogers,
In the Clerk's Office of the District Court of the United States,
In and for the Eastern District of Pennsylvania.

{ Northern lithograph, 1861 }

THE CONFEDERACY, again personified as Jefferson Davis, was still growing. The original seven states that had seceded prior to Lincoln's inauguration believed that others naturally belonged within their ranks. Two in particular, Tennessee and Virginia, were being actively courted by officials of the new government from Montgomery.

Having been portrayed as a thief in the night, Davis was now pictured as a fox on this patriotic envelope, attempting to steal these two fat geese and bring them to Dixie's land.

When Confederate forces in Charleston opened a bombardment on the Federal garrison in Fort Sumter in early April 1861, Lincoln called for seventy-five thousand volunteers for the army to subdue the growing rebellion. The call for volunteers was the catalyst. Within a week, Virginia seceded. She was followed within weeks by Arkansas and North Carolina. Tennessee finally joined the Confederacy in June.

The players were now all in place, and the great, bloody confrontation was about to begin.

JEFF. DAVIS ON A SCOUTING EXPEDITION

{ Patriotic envelope, 1861 }

THE WAR, and all that was about to happen, was Lincoln's fault, according to this Southern cartoon.

It is Lincoln, in the costume of a fool, who is at the center of this stage of death (symbolized by the skeleton) and of war (symbolized by the military musical instruments and the prone soldier at right). He is surrounded by mere puppets in the form of Secretary of War Simon Cameron and Secretary of the Navy Gideon Welles, and Generals John C. Frémont, Winfield Scott, George McClellan, and Benjamin Butler.

Backstage, behind the scene, is Secretary of the Treasury Salmon P. Chase. As producer of this comedy, he had the job of raising the funds necessary for its execution.

Lincoln was demonized in the South. As head of the "Black Republicans," that group in government under the influence of the abolitionists and dedicated to the eradication of states' rights in general and slavery in particular, he came to personify all that was wrong with a strong central government. Such a government, it was believed, would trample the rights of individuals and legitimate local authority. It would spell the end of liberty (white man's liberty, of course).

Thus, it was the prevalent political belief among Southerners that voluntary withdrawal from such a centralized government was a prudent course of action—indeed, the only course of action available—if individual rights were to be preserved. This severing of political ties and affiliation with the federal government, therefore, was an act of patriotism, not at all unlike the steps their fathers and grandfathers had taken by severing their ties with King George III of England nearly a century earlier. In Confederate eyes, this was to be a war for Southern independence, and a second American Revolution.

THE COMEDY OF DEATH

{ *Aldabert Volck,* July 1861 }

JEFF DAVIS REAPING THE HARVEST

{ Harper's Weekly, October 26, 1861 }

CCORDING TO this *Harper's Weekly* cartoon, Davis bore full responsibility for the war and the destruction it caused.

Davis is portrayed here as a ghoul, working as a harvester of death. He works at night surrounded by the symbols of death: the hangman's noose and the waiting vulture, with still more vultures on the horizon and approaching quickly. The work of the South, as personified by Davis, is to yield only more death. He has only just started gathering his crop for harvesting, but there is more to be had at his hands.

Just as Lincoln was demonized in the South, Davis was cast in the role of a devil by the North. He assumed the qualities of all that was wrong with the concept of the Confederate States of America. He had turned his back on his country, and that was treason. He had ended any chances of a peaceful, political solution by assuming unreasonable stands and by taking the wholly unjustified step of seceding from a holy union. And he had started a war by firing upon his country's flag at Fort Sumter.

The artist portrays a grim and dark image. It foreshadows the growing Northern acceptance that the war would not be pleasant nor would it pass quickly.

Harper's Weekly pictured the Northern blockade of Southern ports as an unexpected ingredient in the South's plans.

Jefferson Davis, embodying the South, is surprised when he receives his "smash" from a Federal hand. (Smash, by the way, was a traditional libation of the South. Similar to a julep, it consisted of bourbon or rum, sugar, and mint served over crushed ice in a small glass.) This drink contains a fresh ingredient, Northern warships, and Davis does not appear pleased. Nor do his generals, pictured behind him (from left: Robert E. Lee, Pierre Gustave Toutant Beauregard, and Joseph E. Johnston).

Lincoln had actually imposed the blockade in April, immediately after Virginia seceded. At its inception, it was more of a nuisance than a hindrance, since the Union navy did not have nearly enough ships to enforce its decree. On the other hand, the Confederate navy existed only in an office in Richmond, with virtually no ships at all.

Lincoln would eventually authorize the commissioning of more than five hundred vessels to enforce the blockade. They would patrol the Atlantic coast and the Gulf of Mexico in search of Confederate or neutral ships carrying trade goods or war matériel. The South responded with blockade-runners, small, fast ships designed to haul cargo rather than do battle.

The primary success of the blockade was in shutting down neutral shipping. It has been estimated that five out of six blockade-runners made successful trips to either the Bahamas or Cuba, but the necessity for speed drastically reduced the tonnage each blockade-runner could carry. Although hazardous, the trips were lucrative for their captains and crews; however, the relatively small amount of goods brought in did little to improve conditions in the South.

A "SMASH" FOR JEFF

{ *Harper's Weekly*, November 2, 1861 }

CAPTURE OF SECESSION VARMINTS.

BULL—"What are you about, sir? Picking pockets, eh?"
JONATHAN—"Don't get wrathy, now! You shouldn't be carryin' skunks about with you, John!"
(And Jonathan necks the varmints accordingly)

{ *Leslie's Illustrated*, December 7, 1861 }

MORALE ON THE Northern home front received a much needed boost late in the year when Confederate emissaries to England and France were captured on the high seas.

John Slidell and James M. Mason had been appointed special commissioners of the Confederate government. Their mission was to travel to Europe in order to plead the case of the Confederacy. They hoped for diplomatic recognition and aid. Running the blockade, they transferred aboard a British ship, the *Trent,* for passage. Word of their mission and their itinerary reached Captain Charles Wilkes, of the *San Jacinto.* Lying in wait, he stopped the *Trent* in international waters in November 1861 and forcibly removed the Confederates. The two were then imprisoned in Boston.

Leslie's Illustrated portrays the emissaries as skunks, and the United States, personified as Brother Jonathan, as doing a favor for Great Britain by removing them.

The boost to Northern morale was short-lived. The act was wholly illegal, and it triggered an international incident. Great Britain issued the most serious protests possible and threatened war against the United States, going so far as to send an army to Canada in preparation for an invasion.

ACCORDING TO *Punch,* Colonel Bull (Great Britain) had the Yankee raccoon (Lincoln) in his sights with nowhere to run over the *Trent* affair. The United States had violated international law by removing two Confederate emissaries from a British ship on the high seas.

As much as Lincoln needed a victory for the Northern war effort (and he very much did after the string of debacles the Union had suffered during the year), he was forced to concede that Great Britain was in the right. What Wilkes had done in removing the Confederates was plainly in violation of international law.

Several members of Lincoln's cabinet, most notably Secretary of State William Seward, favored going to war with Great Britain. His reasoning was that if the United States were threatened by an outside force, the South would rejoin the Union to defend against the common foe. Lincoln disagreed.

"One war at a time," he told Seward as he directed that Mason and Slidell should be sent on their way and appropriate assurances given to Her Majesty's government in London. *Punch* saw it as Lincoln's admission of guilt.

"UP A TREE."—COLONEL BULL AND THE YANKEE 'COON.

'COON: "Air you in earnest, Colonel?"
COLONEL BULL: "I am."
'COON: "Don't fire—I'll come down."

{ *Punch*, January 1862 }

A SHORT BLANKET

OLD SECESH. "While I cover my neck, I expose my feet, and if I cover my feet, I expose my neck. Ugh!"

{ *Harper's Weekly,* December 14, 1861 }

IN THE FALL of 1861, many Unionists believed that the Confederate army was in a most uncomfortable position, with too many demands on too few resources. It needed to protect Virginia and its port cities of Savannah in Georgia and Charleston in South Carolina. There was little comfort, according to *Harper's Weekly,* to be found in the too short blanket that was the army of the "Confederated States." No matter where the blanket was moved, something vital would be exposed.

The Confederate military could not possibly defend its entire territory. On the other hand, at this point in the war, it didn't need to. The Union armies had done little to threaten vast stretches of the Confederacy.

Overall command of Federal forces had passed from Winfield Scott to Major General George McClellan. In the East, McClellan was transforming a group of short-term volunteers into a professional army. He spent the greater part of the first year of the war training, reorganizing, and resupplying the Army of the Potomac. He gave it a name and an identity. He gave it, and the folks at home, something to take pride in.

While Lincoln recognized the need to build a professional force, he became increasingly frustrated with "Little Mac," as McClellan was called by the troops, because he knew that rebel forces were making use of the time to do exactly the same. The difference was that the Confederates were working on defense, while the Federals were working toward offense.

Scholars have argued that the Confederacy actually had an easier job during the war, since it would be defending its home territory. Union forces, on the other hand, would have to conquer and hold a vast and hostile territory. Lines of supply and communication would be stretched. Reinforcements would be difficult to send where needed. And while the Federals would have the advantages of manpower and resources, the rebels would have advantages of their own, not the least of which was their cause. It could, therefore, be argued that the Confederacy didn't need a large blanket to protect vital areas.

Lofty principles of states' rights may not have been a powerful and energizing factor for many Southerners. Fighting off an invader, one bent on the destruction of their homes, their families, and their livelihoods, on the other hand, was a very real and concrete motivation. At this point in the war, the North was fighting for an abstract ideal, one of preserving the Union. While that may have inspired patriotic songs and politicians' speeches, it was hardly the stuff that would make the citizen-soldier son of a Pennsylvania farmer look forward to yet another night sleeping in the mud.

All the Confederates had to do was survive. The Federals, on the other hand, had to prevail. The two tasks were significantly different.

ACCORDING TO this cartoon published in *Harper's Weekly* in early 1862, the *Richmond Examiner* provided evidence of the stranglehold the North had on the South. McClellan and his armies are the snake, squeezing the life out of the Confederacy. Jefferson Davis, with horns, appears to be in agony while Confederate forces struggle to break free of the vise grip. This cartoon seems to reinforce the Northern view of the overwhelming strength of Federal forces.

McClellan had taken his Army of the Potomac deep into Virginia. Landing his forces unopposed at the tip of land between the James and York rivers, he began a march up the Virginia Peninsula to take the Confederate capital in Richmond. It would bring, he hoped, a swift and relatively bloodless end to the war.

Reinforcements had swept in from throughout the Confederacy to defend the capital. But although it seemed to the public that the city's defenses were formidable, they were not.

McClellan's intelligence service, led by detective Allan Pinkerton, told him that the Confederates outnumbered him nearly two to one (when in fact, just the opposite was true). McClellan cried for reinforcements from Washington and proceeded slowly. When he ran into resistance from rebel forces, he fell back. The Northern press called it a masterful retreat and a magnificent logistical performance.

LITTLE MAC'S UNION SQUEEZE

"At the moment we find ourselves in the face of superior forces wherever we look, whether to the North, the East or the West or the South itself. Generals JOSEPH JOHNSTON and BEAU-REGARD are held by McClellan on the Potomac as in a vice."—*Richmond Examiner*, January 16.

{ *Harper's Weekly*, February 8, 1862 }

{ *Aldabert J. Volck, Summer 1862* }

THE ONLY MAN as vilified by the South as Abraham Lincoln was Major General Benjamin Butler, portrayed here as Sancho Panza, the ignorant and bumbling sidekick to Lincoln's absurd Don Quixote.

Butler was a War Democrat from Massachusetts and a popular politician at the start of the war. It was he who led troops into Baltimore, and trained artillery on the city, in order to subdue the citizens and keep Maryland in the Union during the early days. It was he who, as a rationale for contravening provisions of the fugitive slave law, coined the phrase "contraband of war" to describe escaped slaves. And it was Butler who was named the military administrator of New Orleans after the city surrendered to Federal forces in April 1862.

It was in New Orleans that he earned the sobriquet "Spoons Butler," a reference to rumors that he personally confiscated property belonging to rebel sympathizers.

And it was also in New Orleans that he became known as "Beast Butler" after he issued his General Order No. 28. The order attempted to address the abuse that was being heaped upon his officers by ladies of the city who were still loyal to the Confederacy. At first much of the disrespect was harmless (crossing the street when an officer approached or gathering skirts and turning their backs upon officers), but the incidents escalated. Women would spit upon Federal soldiers, and teach their children to do the same. Up to that point, Federal officers had acted with restraint, but Butler feared a serious retaliatory incident might take place. So he issued his order, which said, in part,

when any female shall, by word, gesture, or movement, insult or show contempt for any officer or soldier of the United States, she shall be regarded and held liable to be treated as a woman of the town plying her avocation.

The resulting outcry (from the South) was universal. Jefferson Davis issued a proclamation calling Butler a criminal, and ordering his immediate execution should he be captured. New chamber pots, featuring Butler's portrait at the business end, were soon available in New Orleans. And "Spoons Butler" became "Beast Butler."

After a few women were actually jailed for ignoring the order, the insults tapered off and eventually stopped.

FOLLOWING McClellan's masterful retreat, Lincoln turned his attention to Major General John Pope, putting him in command of a newly constituted army. Pope, it was hoped, would get things moving in the East. In one of his first moves, Pope issued orders saying that the war would now be prosecuted in earnest (implying that up to that point neither side had been serious). According to this cartoon in *Harper's Weekly,* the Confederacy was insulted by Pope's insinuations.

In fact, the rebel army, now dubbed the Army of Northern Virginia by its new commanding officer, Robert E. Lee, had already begun to "carry on the war in earnest." The army was on the move with the intent of invading the North. It would meet Pope a little more than twenty miles outside Washington, D.C., at the town of Manassas, Virginia, on the same ground where the First Battle of Bull Run had been fought the previous year. There, at the Second Battle of Bull Run (or Second Manassas, as the Confederates styled it), Pope was soundly defeated. The Federals again were thrown back, and the Confederates continued on to Maryland.

SCENE, GENERAL HEAD-QUARTERS, RICHMOND.

REBEL GENERAL (*reading* GENERAL POPE's *Orders*). "What! going to carry on the War in earnest! Here, JONES, SMITH, BROWN, all of you, ride at once to JACKSON, and order him to hang the Sconndrel POPE at once! Chop his Head off! Roast him on a slow Fire! Crucify him!"

{ *Harper's Weekly*, August 30, 1862 }

"NOT UP TO TIME;"

Or, Interference would be very Welcome.

{ *Punch*, September 13, 1862 }

RANCE, in the form of a slightly portly eagle, and Great Britain, in the form of a worried-looking lion, wonder if it is time to intervene in this war, especially since the participants appear to be made weary by the fight. In this cartoon, which appeared less than a week before the Battle of Antietam, *Punch* thought that both sides were nearly played out.

Neither of the two European powers had taken an official position, although both were keenly interested in the outcome, and both leaned toward recognition of the Confederate States of America.

Great Britain wanted to resume imports of the South's cotton. Its supplies were running low and its textile mills were beginning to lay off workers. The resulting unemployment was not healthy for its economy. At the same time, it was importing wheat from the North and needed an uninterrupted supply. So Great Britain was hesitant to pick one side over the other until it was sure which would win.

France also wanted a resumption of shipments of cotton. But at least as important were its designs on Mexico. France wanted to establish a puppet government there and hoped, as an ally of the South, that it would be permitted to do so without interference. Still, it did not want to anger the North, just in case the Federals won. So France looked to Great Britain to take the lead.

There was talk of calling for a peace conference, with the Europeans acting as mediators. If the North did not go along (and it had already said it would not), both sides could then recognize the South and, perhaps, intervene. All they needed was to be shown that the South could win. All they needed was a significant Southern victory.

ROBERT E. LEE and his Army of Northern Virginia invaded the North. In a strategic move designed to relieve the pressure on Richmond and demonstrate their ability to threaten Northern cities, the Confederates had crossed the Potomac River from Virginia into Maryland in September 1862. Lee had hoped to be greeted by secession-leaning Marylanders as liberators. *Harper's Weekly* reflected the disappointment of Maryland at the sight of the army.

The Army of Northern Virginia had taken on mythic status in portions of the Union, particularly in those areas with decidedly Southern sympathies. They were seen to be invincible, honorable, and noble warriors, while at the same time being both gallant and cavalier gentlemen. They had met the Federal armies and beaten them back with seeming ease. And now the rebels had turned and were becoming the invader rather than the invaded.

But the reality was different from the glorified vision. Some elements of the army had been in the field for more than a year at this point. Supplies were running low and deprivations were beginning to show.

Lee had several reasons for bringing his army north. The first, purely practical reason, was that he needed to resupply. Provisions of all kind—food, munitions, clothing, and horses—were running low, and he hoped to secure more in Maryland. He had reason to hope for a cordial reception from the people there. The state was below the Mason-Dixon Line and its sympathies were with the South (it had sent as many men to the Confederate army as it had to the Union army).

A second reason was to curry the favor of Great Britain and France. If it could be shown that the Confederate armies were viable (by capturing a Federal city like Baltimore, for example), then Europe would call for a peace conference and might, conceivably, join the war on the side of the South. The invasion was an attempt to show Europe that the South was viable.

And so Lee and his army came. They did not look as glorious, perhaps, as supporters in Maryland had envisioned. But they were not yet as bedraggled as *Harper's Weekly* portrayed them.

THE REBEL CHIVALRY

As the fancy of "My Maryland" painted them. As "My Maryland" found them.

{ *Harper's Weekly*, October 4, 1862 }

"Now, Marshall, sing us 'Picayune Butler', or something else that's funny."

{ Northern broadside, Fall 1862 *}*

THIS BROADSIDE, printed in the fall of 1862, purports to represent the scene when Lincoln went among the battlefield wounded in Sharpsburg, Maryland.

On September 17, 1862, the two great armies met near the town of Sharpsburg, along the banks of Antietam Creek, in what was to be the single bloodiest day of the war. Casualties totaled more than twenty thousand. The Confederates lost nearly one-third of their forces; the Federals, nearly 25 percent. Tactically the battle was a draw, but the Union could claim a strategic victory, since Lee was forced to withdraw his forces back into Virginia, thus ending the first Confederate invasion of the North. The country was horrified by the casualty figures.

Lincoln visited the battlefield later in the month, and that gave rise to one of the uglier rumors of the war. It was said that during his battlefield tour Lincoln told jokes and laughed while wounded still lay on the ground around him. The story was reported in the Northern press, and morale in the North was low enough that these reports were given credence.

COLUMBIA, symbol of the mothers, wives, and sweethearts of the nation's soldiers, demands an accounting for the thousands dead in Fredericksburg, Virginia. *Harper's Weekly,* in this early 1863 cartoon, demands an explanation.

The war was not going well for the North, and Lincoln was increasingly being criticized for Union defeats. Lincoln, according to the artist, tries to respond with a joke. Secretary of War Edwin Stanton and Major General Henry Halleck, commanding general of all the Union armies, stand helplessly at Lincoln's side. It is Lincoln who is ultimately responsible.

According to the artist, the country was tired of the jokes and growing tired of Lincoln, as well. "Go tell your joke at Springfield [Lincoln's hometown in Illinois]!" he is told.

Following the bloody battle at Antietam, Lincoln replaced McClellan with Major General Ambrose Burnside. Following the disaster at Fredericksburg, Burnside was replaced with Major General "Fighting Joe" Hooker, who was in command during the Union disaster at Chancellorsville, Virginia. Hooker was then replaced by Major General George Meade.

COLUMBIA. "Where are my 15,000 sons—murdered at Fredericksburg?"

LINCOLN. "This reminds me of a little joke—"

COLUMBIA. "Go tell your joke at Springfield!!"

{ *Harper's Weekly*, January 3, 1863 }

Lincoln's Dreams, or, There's a Good Time Coming

{ Leslie's Illustrated, February 14, 1863 *}*

WHILE *Harper's Weekly* blamed Lincoln for the string of disasters, in this cartoon *Leslie's Illustrated* suggests Lincoln's subordinates are to blame. In February 1863, now nearly two years into a war that most supposed would last ninety days, fixing blame was a common topic of conversation.

After a string of Union generals have already been beheaded, Lincoln dreams of others who may be brought to answer for the failed course of the war. According to the artist, Generals Pope (Bull Run), McClellan (Peninsula campaign), and Burnside (Fredericksburg) have already been to the chopping block. Next in line is Secretary of State William Seward, followed by Edwin Stanton, recently appointed secretary of war, and Gideon Welles, secretary of the navy. General Halleck stands at the end of the line.

Is there no one, the artist wonders, Lincoln can trust to correct events?

By late February 1863, *Leslie's Illustrated* was calling Lincoln a mudsill.

Even if he wasn't to blame for the long and growing string of disastrous battles, Lincoln was still stuck in the mud and Davis was still safe and happy, out of reach in Richmond. It seemed that all Lincoln could do was stand and rail against him.

By definition, a mudsill is the lowest part of the foundation, usually a block of wood, which sits between the mud and the foundation of the building. In mid-nineteenth-century America, a "mudsill" was the lowest member of society. The mudsill was the one who did all the menial labor that allowed the upper classes of society to prosper. Many Southerners and plantation owners believed in mudsill "theory," arguing that slaves, or the lower classes, existed for the upper classes, that they were willing to perform the tasks necessary to advance the upper classes.

As a mudsill, then, Lincoln's labor would go to enrich an employer rather than build wealth for himself, and this was scorned by the better classes. In calling Lincoln a mudsill, the artist suggests that Lincoln was doing the bulk of the work but getting nothing out of it for himself.

The Bad Bird and the Mudsill

{ *Leslie's Illustrated*, February 21, 1863 }

LINCOLN'S TWO DIFFICULTIES

{ *Punch*, August 23, 1862 }

MEN AND MONEY. Lincoln needed more of both. According to *Punch,* he was caught squarely between the two.

Financing the war was becoming a real problem. Receipts for the government's coffers had fallen dramatically with the coming of the war. Prior to the war, the vast majority of government revenue came from tariffs imposed on imported goods, and much of that came from goods arriving in Southern ports. With the blockade of the South in place, imports had been eliminated, and that source of revenue vanished.

At the same time, demands upon the Treasury had never been higher. Active armies and navies were consumers of resources—equipment, provisions, payroll. All cost money that the government simply did not have.

One alternative was to print money, and this the government did. The first greenbacks were issued during the Civil War. But left uncontrolled, this practice would quickly lead to rampant inflation of prices and a corresponding devaluation of currency. This was exactly what was happening with Confederate currency.

The government in Washington needed to control the amount of money in circulation. It did this in two ways: first, it restricted the amount of money being printed; and second, it removed as much money as it could from the hands of the population by instituting the first income tax. Not only did the tax curtail inflation, it also helped replace revenue lost by the reduction of tariff receipts. Nearly everyone won—except, of course, those who now had to begin paying income tax.

The problem of staffing the armies had been left to the states, but a more systematic approach was required. A military draft was imposed by both the North and the South. It would prove to be as unpopular as the income tax.

IN WHAT MAY BE the first joke made at the expense of federal tax collectors, *Leslie's Illustrated* imagines a visit to the home of a typical taxpayer. The Federal government, it appears, will begin to look into all aspects of domestic life. Not content merely to take a man's watch, these dour men swarm through the house checking bedclothes, looking under the bed, and even examining what may be beneath hoopskirts.

But a way had been found to finance the war. It was all in the cause of preserving the Union.

THE HOME OF THE AMERICAN CITIZEN AFTER THE TAX BILL HAS PASSED.

N.B.—Scroggs says he is ready and willing to pay any amount of tax, but he would like them to leave his wife's crinoline and other domestic trifles alone.

{ *Leslie's Illustrated*, June 1863 }

NEARLY THREE YEARS into the war, Lincoln may have finally found the right tool for the job. He sits and contemplates this latest broom, labeled "Grant." He had already gone through a number of different tools, the artist notes. Scattered on the floor behind Lincoln's chair are broken brooms labeled "Pope," "McLellan," and "Hooker."

Ulysses S. Grant was a general from the West, where he had scored earlier victories with the capture of Fort Henry and Fort Donaldson, but rumors of his drinking had hampered his rise. He was in command at Shiloh, another Union victory. Then he went on to capture Vicksburg, which returned the Mississippi River to Federal control. Assuming command of the beleaguered Army of the Cumberland at Chattanooga, he broke a siege and routed a Confederate army under General Braxton Bragg.

Grant may have been the tool that the Union required.

MR. LINCOLN FINDS A BROOM TO HIS LIKING.

{ *Leslie's Illustrated,* March 7, 1864 }

IN JULY 1863, draft riots broke out in New York City ("Gotham" in this *Leslie's Illustrated* cartoon). For the better part of a week, mobs composed primarily of Irish and German immigrants went on the rampage throughout Manhattan. After setting fire to a number of public buildings and landmarks, the mob irrationally turned its wrath on African-Americans. Innocent men, women, and children were dragged from their homes, beaten, and, in some cases, lynched on the street. Troops were finally moved from the recent battlefield in Gettysburg, Pennsylvania, and brought to the city to restore order. By the time the riots were quelled, more than a thousand people were dead. Similar reactions, although not nearly as violent, took place in Chicago and Cincinnati.

The riots had been triggered by the new draft imposed by the Federal government. More than two years into the war, the ranks of both armies were becoming depleted. Enlistments had been completed. Desertions were on the rise. And, of course, casualties were taking their toll.

Both sides instituted a draft. Reactions from the home fronts were swift and negative. Many in the North who were due to be drafted were newly arrived immigrants, who had sacrificed much just to make the journey to America. They were now being forced to take part in a war they did not really understand. The intangible goal of "Union" meant little. The notion of freeing slaves, who would then compete for jobs, was not compelling. Thus, they could see their dreams of new lives and new opportunities for their families disappearing in the black-powder smoke of gunfire. Despite the riots, by the end of the war in April 1865, the Union had more than a million men under arms and in the field, and another 2.25 million men registered and on standby status.

THE NAUGHTY BOY GOTHAM, WHO WOULD NOT TAKE THE DRAFT

MAMMY LINCOLN: "There now, you bad boy, acting that way,
when your little sister Penn takes hers like a baby."

{ *Leslie's Illustrated*, August 29, 1863 }

SCENE, FIFTH AVENUE.

He. "Ah! Dearest Addie! I've succeeded. I've got a Substitute!"
She. "Have you? What a curious coincidence! And *I* have found one for YOU!"

(Harper's Weekly, August 30, 1863)

LTHOUGH HIRING a substitute to take your place in the ranks was perfectly legal, it perhaps wasn't the wisest course of action, according to this cartoon from *Harper's Weekly*. The young lady, rather than being pleased that the gentleman has found a substitute, has decided to find a substitute of her own.

The business of finding and hiring substitutes gave substance to the charges in the North that this was a rich man's war but a poor man's fight. The cost of a substitute, $300, was equal to nearly a year's pay for the working class. Quite obviously, it was not a sum they were prepared to pay. For the upper echelons of society, on the other hand, it was a reasonable amount.

The system spawned an industry in the brokering of substitutes. For a small fee, in addition to the $300, the broker would find a man to act as substitute. Often these men were either physically or mentally challenged and were not fit for active duty. But the substitute brokers would find a way to bribe them into the army.

Yet another industry arose among those who acted as substitutes. They would stay just long enough to collect their bounties. They would then desert, move to another town, and, under another name, start the process yet again.

Many hired substitutes to avoid active service. (Lincoln himself had one.) But the system was a failure. General Grant said that not one in eight was worth having in the ranks.

THE UNION had a source of untapped recruits in the African-Americans living within Federal lines. Many were free men. And many were contrabands, former slaves who had escaped from Southern masters.

In this *Punch* cartoon, the artist depicts a would-be recruit as aloof and unwilling, but this was exactly opposite of the truth. Particularly after Lincoln issued his Emancipation Proclamation, the ranks of volunteers swelled with black recruits. Between 1863 and 1865, more than 180,000 African-Americans joined the army.

Their path had not been easy. Early on, Lincoln had urged their enlistment, but he met with stiff resistance from his cabinet and from officers of the regular army. Any African-Americans attached to the army were civilians, and served as cooks, servants, and manual laborers.

With the fall of Vicksburg and the opening of the Mississippi River in the summer of 1863, attitudes changed. While still possessing a field command in the West, Grant wrote to Lincoln urging any restrictions be lifted. "We have added a powerful ally," he wrote. "They will make good soldiers, and taking them from the enemy weakens him in the same proportion they strengthen us."

Units were segregated with black soldiers serving under white officers. But serve they did in every major campaign from the autumn months of 1863 through the end of the war.

ONE GOOD TURN DESERVES ANOTHER.

"Why, I du decalre, it's my dear old friend Sambo. Lend us a hand, old boos, du."

{ *Punch*, August 9, 1862 }

· 4 ·

THE PECULIAR
INSTITUTION

The Issues of Slavery

THE CENTRAL ISSUE of the Civil War was chattel slavery. There were other issues, such as notions of the rights of individual states and the continuation of the Union, but the one problem that could no longer be resolved through political negotiation and compromise was the question of the continued existence of slavery within the United States.

Slavery was made legal by the Constitution of the United States. It was further reinforced by the Supreme Court in its 1857 ruling in *Dred Scott v. Sanford.* That ruling said, in part, that Congress did not have the power to restrict slavery in federal territories. The law of the land, therefore, said that slavery could continue to expand.

The South, however, feared the growing dominance of the North. With its growing population fueling industrial and financial wealth, and an infrastructure of railroads connecting urban manufacturing centers with rich agricultural lands, the North was in position to overwhelm the South's primarily agrarian society. The South's only advantage lay in the availability of slave labor. It feared the North's increasing hostility against the "peculiar institution."

It was not a simple issue. Slave owners in the South were in the minority. But the entire economy revolved around slavery. The wealth of the South was in property—both land and slaves. An attack on slavery would be an attack on the underpinnings of the Southern economy and its entire way of life.

At the same time, there was a growing uneasiness in the North over what would happen to the newly freed slaves. Would this population now migrate to the North and compete for jobs in the factories? Would these uneducated and largely unskilled masses overwhelm Northern society?

Although volume upon volume is written to prove slavery a very good thing, we never hear of the man who wishes to take the good of it, by being a slave himself.

—Abraham Lincoln, 1854

Harper's Weekly neatly sums up a host of complex and many-layered issues in this prewar cartoon.

A well-dressed African-American freely walking the streets was a threat to established societal norms of both North and South. In the North, if a black man could afford to be nattily dressed, it meant that he had a job, a job that would otherwise have gone to a white man. In the South, if a black man was at his leisure, it meant that he was not a slave. In either case, it was a crisis.

In the prejudiced and strictly segregated American society of the mid-nineteenth century, the presence of African-Americans was a significant factor in the dissolution of the Union. Slavery was the single overriding issue of the day. Radical abolitionists were demanding its immediate end. Radical secessionists were demanding its unhindered extension to the western territories; some wanted to go even further by annexing Cuba and other islands in the Caribbean as slave territory. Northern moderates were wary of the political power the South had in Washington. Southern moderates were just as wary of encroachments on their way of life.

But the issues went deeper still. While many in the North opposed the very notion of slavery, not all believed the practice was evil. And in the South, where only a small percentage of the population actually owned slaves, not everyone believed the practice should continue. There was disagreement, too, on what was to be done with a liberated black population. Charitable societies were founded to sponsor the return of blacks to Africa. Lincoln himself championed the movement to found new colonies of former slaves in Central America. There were movements to ban the resettlement of freed slaves from the South to the North.

In 1800, the black population of the country totaled roughly a million; by 1860, the population had increased to nearly 4 million. If this population was no longer in bondage, its members might easily become competitors for jobs in the North. The Mid-Atlantic and New England states were already experiencing rapid population growth through mass immigration. The Irish and Germans, in particular, were inundating the cities of the North looking for work. More competition from a newly freed labor force was not welcome. And a crisis was, indeed, upon the land.

"Hello BILL! there goes the CRISIS!"

{ *Harper's Weekly*, February 2, 1861 }

(North)—A Fish Out of Water.

(South)—UNCLE CLEM. "Say, Massa Jim, is I wan of them onfuntunate Niggers as you was reading about?"

YOUNG GENTLEMAN. "Yes, Clem, you are one of them."

UNCLE CLEM. "Well, it's a great pity about me. I'se berry badly off, I is."

{ *Harper's Weekly,* January 26, 1861 }

THE IDEA that slaves were somehow better off than freemen is perpetuated in this offering by *Harper's Weekly*. The artist seems to suggest that slaves may, indeed, be better off in their present lot than they would be as freemen in the North.

In the North (left panel), the African-American is dressed in rags, and inadequately at that, as he plods through the snow past a warm and inviting establishment. Not only is he cold, he is also unwelcome. He is projected as "a fish out of water," alone and perhaps close to destitute.

In contrast, the right panel shows the happy-go-lucky slave as comfortably dressed, with a pipe, who doesn't appear to be working too hard as he and his "Massa" discuss the news of the day. In the background another slave appears to be heading toward the fishing hole as children play. It is a bucolic scene, one that is not designed to inspire pity for the poor slave who doesn't know how "berry badly off" he is.

IN 1859, the exploits of Blondin, a French gymnast and performer, captivated and distracted the country. Already famous in Europe, Blondin (whose real name was Jean-François Gravelet) undertook a tour of the United States and performed dazzling feats of acrobatics to packed houses in major cities. By way of promotion, he performed a number of hair-raising stunts for the benefit of the newspapers. He stretched a tightrope across Niagara Falls, for example, and made a number of crossings, with each being just a little more spectacular than the last. First, he'd push a wheelbarrow across. Then he'd carry someone on his back. Finally, he'd sit down at the halfway mark and have lunch.

So it was shortly after Lincoln received the Republican nomination that *Vanity Fair* made this comparison. Rather than a tightrope, Lincoln the rail-splitter was making the perilous trip to the White House (seen in the left background) by walking along a rather rickety rail, and he is doing it while encumbered by a black child.

While the Republican Party was generally seen as extolling the abolitionist cause, Lincoln himself did not endorse an immediate end to slavery. While he was personally against the practice, he saw no way under the Constitution to bring it to an end. Lincoln's primary focus was to preserve the Union. Perhaps this is what the artist had in mind when he placed Horace Greeley, ardent abolitionist and publisher of the *New York Tribune,* in the right background telling Lincoln, "Don't drop the carpet-bag." Greeley, like many other abolitionists, feared that Lincoln would abandon Republican principles of emancipation in order to keep the South from seceding.

SHAKY.

DARING TRANSIT ON THE PERILOUS RAIL,   · · · · ·   Mr. Abraham Blondin De Lave Lincoln.

{ Vanity Fair, June 9, 1860 }

THE AMERICAN DIFFICULTY

PRESIDENT ABE: What a nice White House this would be, if it were not for the blacks!

{*Punch*, May 11, 1861}

UNAWARE THAT Lincoln had grown a beard, this London *Punch* artist shows him clean-shaven (a mistake that would not be repeated) shortly after his inauguration. Lincoln appears in the Executive Mansion, as it was formally known at the time, stoking a fire as smoke billows and cinders fall around him. "What a nice White House this would be," he says, "if it were not for the blacks." Now that he was president, Lincoln had a difficult job to do, and the world was waiting and watching to see how he would handle it.

Lincoln believed his job was to preserve the Union. Everything else was secondary to that task. While the notion of slavery was repugnant to him, and he very much wanted to end the practice, he would have accepted its continuance if by so doing he could preserve the Union.

During his first inaugural address, he spoke directly to the people of the South when he said, "I have no purpose, directly or indirectly, to interfere with the institution of slavery in the States where it exists. I believe I have no lawful right to do so, and I have no inclination to do so." The problem was that few, if any, believed him.

At that point, the Confederate States of America had already been established. It had a government, a constitution, a president, and an army of its own. Lincoln, elected by the North, was president of a divided country.

The world, not just the country, watched and wondered how Lincoln would deal with this "American difficulty." What would he do about this problem of "the blacks"?

IT APPEARED, later that summer, that Lincoln would distance himself from the question of slavery when he was forced to revoke a proclamation of emancipation that had been issued by Major General John C. Frémont.

Frémont had been given command of Federal forces in the West, an area that included Missouri, a state teetering toward anarchy. Secessionist guerrilla forces were terrorizing the population. In his capacity as military governor of the state, Frémont believed slave labor to be an aid to his enemy, and in August 1861 he issued a proclamation declaring all slaves within the state were "forever free." He didn't have the authority, nor did he bother to inform Lincoln of his move.

It was problematic for a number of reasons. The war had not been going well for the Federals at that point, and Lincoln was hardly in a position of either political or military strength. At the same time, the stated goal of the war was to preserve the Union, not to free the slaves. No fewer than three of the states that had remained in the Union—Kentucky, Maryland, and Delaware—allowed slavery within their borders. Lincoln desperately needed the support of those states, but if it appeared that the aim of the war was to free the slaves, that support would evaporate.

So Lincoln was put in the position of having to revoke Frémont's proclamation. Within weeks, Frémont was relieved of his command. The border states did not bolt from the Union, but Lincoln was put in the position, as depicted here, of appearing to abandon the principles of abolition.

Leslie's Illustrated pictures Lincoln adrift and floundering through this storm. With Frémont's proclamation floating past, Lincoln is pushing a slave away, since the Union life preserver cannot save them both.

LINCOLN—"*I'm sorry to have to drop you, Sambo, but this concern won't carry us both!*"

{ *Leslie's Illustrated*, October 12, 1861 }

JOHN BULL—Helloa, Dr. Livingstone, this is a rather slim crop for ten years, you know.

{ Leslie's Illustrated, December 28, 1861 *}*

THE BLOCKADE of Confederate ports that had been imposed by the government in Washington during the opening summer of the war was viewed by the Northern press as having an effect on the European economy. *Leslie's Illustrated* reflected that view in this cartoon showing John Bull (the personification of Great Britain) complaining that their alternative source for cotton, Africa, wasn't producing the crop that had been promised.

Great Britain found itself in a most uncomfortable position as a result of the American conflict. The economy of Great Britain, and to a lesser extent France, was being transformed by the Industrial Revolution. Much of the growth was being funded by the textile mills. The mills required cotton as a raw ingredient, and most of the world's cotton came from the area now calling itself the Confederate States of America.

At the same time, the cotton it needed was produced by slave labor. Great Britain had outlawed slavery a generation earlier. So the government could not condone its continuance without being hypocritical. Worse, from the government's point of view, the population of Great Britain was also against the practice, so any attempt to support slavery could have serious political consequences.

The solution would have been alternative sources of cotton. Attempts were being made in Africa and in India. But so far those attempts, as seen here, had been unsuccessful. None could match the output of the American South. John Bull needed a solution.

THE "man with the club," Lincoln, had imposed a blockade upon Southern ports. By its terms, trade with the Confederacy was prohibited. The Federal navy was to patrol Southern waters and intercept any ships attempting to carry goods into or out of Southern ports.

As a practical matter, the navy simply was not up to the task at the start of the war. Too few ships were available to patrol the thousands of miles of coastline. And at the start of the war, at least, the blockade existed only on paper.

Because it did exist on paper, however, the European powers were forced to honor the blockade. If they should attempt to run the blockade they would be, in effect, joining the war on the side of the Confederacy. Although France very much wanted to grant formal recognition to the Confederate States of America and to ignore the blockade, it would not without the connivance of Great Britain. And Great Britain hesitated. As much as Great Britain needed cotton, it was not sure that the Confederate States of America could sustain itself. The Confederacy needed to prove itself viable. So, as is depicted by *Leslie's Illustrated* here, John Bull invites the "individual" at the window of "Davis & C° Dealers in Cotton" to open the door himself. In the meantime, Great Britain would look to India for its cotton.

THE RIVAL COTTON SHOPS

INDIVIDUAL AT WINDOW—Hi! Hi! John Bull, why don't you break the door open
and come see a feller? I've got lots of cotton inside!

JOHN BULL—Well, it don't look 'ealthy. I can get all I want for the present
over the way; so I'll wait till yer open the door yourself, or that man with
the club opens it for you—Au River.

{ *Leslie's Illustrated,* October 5, 1861 }

HOW JEFF DAVIS IS SAVING THE SOUTH.

{ *Harper's Weekly*, April 19, 1862 }

WHILE THE Federal government in Washington was enforcing its blockade, the Confederate government in Richmond was imposing its own embargo. *Harper's Weekly* ran this cartoon, showing Jefferson Davis as a demon in tattered clothing, burning his assets. A slave looks on and it appears that he is ready to flee, with Davis, to Mexico and safety.

In an attempt to prod Great Britain and France into granting diplomatic recognition to the Confederacy as a distinct nation, the South decided to suspend shipment of cotton and tobacco to those countries. The idea was that when the two European powers wanted the goods badly enough, they would take the necessary steps to get them.

It didn't work. In fact, it backfired.

Alternative sources for the goods were already being developed, so Europe would not starve for either commodity. Worse, from the Confederacy's standpoint, these were cash crops that they were refusing to sell. It was upon these that the government's credit was established. Without the crops, there would be no credit. And without the credit, all manner of trade would cease—Union blockade or no. The importation of war matériel, medicines, and consumer and industrial goods was vital to a region that had little or no manufacturing infrastructure. All required payment. And with almost no hard currency and now with no credit, payment was close to impossible.

RHETORIC surrounding the central issue of slavery and African-Americans continued to escalate throughout the war. And cartoonists would use their art in depictions, fair and unfair, of their point of view. Here Baltimore-based caricaturist Aldabert J. Volck voiced aloud the rumors. Under the pseudonym V. Blada (used out of fear of reprisals from Federal authorities), he calls into question Lincoln's true motivations on the question of emancipation and uses a rumor, then in vogue, as his inspiration.

There were many rumors that called into question Lincoln's lineage. His mother had died when we was eight years old. One rumor had it that she had never actually married Lincoln's father. Another said she was of Virginia stock, but of questionable heritage. Many, particularly on the Southern side of the conflict, gave credence to the (incorrect) rumor that Lincoln himself had black blood in his veins. V. Blada drew back the veil of secrecy and "exposed" the true Abraham Lincoln, complete with "Negroid" features.

Although Lincoln himself abhorred slavery and all its trappings, and had since he had witnessed an auction during a trip to New Orleans while still in his twenties, he saw no legal way of putting an end to its practice. It had been repeatedly codified and protected, first in the Constitution and later by a series of rulings by the Supreme Court. His personal belief was that slavery was a moral ill, and that it should be abolished. But his professional belief was that it was legal, and his oath of office (he was sworn to "preserve, protect and defend the Constitution of the United States") prevented him from taking any action.

His inclinations, therefore, were in sympathy with the abolitionists. And while he made no secret of these inclinations, neither did he hide his determination to uphold his oath of office.

But even if his motivations were clear to himself and those closest to him, they were murky, at best, to those who observed his actions from a distance. Throughout the war, dark and persistent whisperings regarding his true motivations were passed from ear to ear.

Jan'y 1864 First appearance in this character (monogram' note)

UNDER THE VEIL

{ V. Blada (Aldabert J. Volck) }

WHO ARE THE NIGGER WORSHIPERS?

Yes, my Son, you must go to War. I can't spare POMP; he cost me Twelve Hundred Dollars, and he might get shot. Besides, you know, you couldn't stoop to work like a field-hand!

{ *Harper's Weekly*, October 18, 1862 }

"A RICH MAN'S WAR and a poor man's fight" is what they called the conflict. The rich, both North and South, had caused this war, they said. And the rich were able to opt out of the armies and battles by paying substitutes to take their places in the ranks. Poor men, who could not afford to hire substitutes, were the ones actually doing the fighting. This was true for both sides.

This *Harper's Weekly* cartoon pointed directly at the owner of the Southern plantation. It was he, the rich slave owner, who caused the war to begin by agitating for secession. He himself wouldn't fight, of course; nor would he allow his slaves to fight (they were far too valuable). He would instead send his son into harm's way.

On one level the artist here is absolutely correct: in economic terms, a slave was far more valuable than a son and was far too valuable to be put at risk on the battlefield.

In 1860, the net worth of the average white male in the South was about $4,000. By contrast, his Northern counterpart's net worth was about half that figure. But the figures are mislead-ing, because the bulk of Southern wealth was in property, particularly land and slaves. Further, the wealth produced by the South's economic output was concentrated in the hands of the slave owners rather than in the hands of the 4 million people who actually did much of the work. And the value of land in the South was declining. Years of single-crop farming had spoiled the South's rich farmland. The value of an acre of Southern farmland, about $10.50, was less than half that of a Northern acre.

One of the reasons the Southern aristocracy rebelled against Northern abolitionists was the very real fear that they would face economic ruin and a total disruption of their social structure if their slaves were suddenly freed and the slave owners were not compensated. It wasn't so much that slaves were viewed as inferior (although they *were* viewed as such), or that Southerners enjoyed keeping them in bondage (although they did enjoy the *profits* of that bond-age). The bulk of Southern wealth was composed of the slaves themselves. If the slaves were suddenly freed, most of the South's wealth would simply walk away.

THERE WAS CAUSE for Northern optimism during the early summer months of 1862, and *Harper's Weekly* provides one, perhaps fanciful, view of Federal progress.

The Army of the Potomac was finally on the move. Major General McClellan had taken the army down the Chesa-peake to the Virginia Peninsula, formed by the James and York rivers. He was steadily advancing up the Peninsula and toward Richmond. With his magnificent army he would soon destroy any Confederates he faced and squash the rebellion. The Confederate army was falling back from Yorktown to defensive posi-

ONE WHO KNOWS HIS OWN VALUE

(A Scene Down South)

MASTER. "Now Johnson, you must have saved a good bit of money. Why don't you purchase your freedom? I will let you have your papers for a comparatively small sum."

JOHNSON. "Well, no, tank you, Sar; fac is, der's so many of des Obbolitionist sogers round, I don' feel like speckelatin' in niggers, jis now."

{ *Harper's Weekly,* July 5, 1862 }

tions around Richmond, and this was seen as proof of McClellan's skill and the imminent end of the war.

That's not the way it worked out, however. During the Seven Days' Battles around Richmond, Confederate general Joseph Johnston was wounded and replaced by a staff officer by the name of Robert E. Lee. When Lee assumed command, he forced McClellan back the way he had come, and the war would continue for three more bloody years.

Still, the work and the goals of the abolitionists ("Obbolitionist sogers") had started to spread among the population of the South—slave and free. Speculation and trade in slaves continued throughout the war years in Richmond and in cities throughout the Confederacy. But it was a business with a definite end in sight.

It was a buyer's market. Slave owners were attempting to protect assets by converting property (i.e., slaves) to cash. There wasn't much cash to be had. Physical currency left over from the prewar period was scarce. There was lit-tle fresh hard currency coming in from foreign trade. And the notes and bonds being issued by the government in Richmond and individual states were viewed with concern in light of the growing inflation. Indeed, the only department within the Confederate government to operate with self-sufficiency throughout the war was the postal service, and that may have been because the value of stamps was fixed. People purchased stamps and used them for trade rather than for postage, so the Post Office Department received the cash for the stamps without having to provide actual service in return.

It was common practice for slaves to earn, and retain, small sums of money for work performed in their spare time for people other than their owners. In rare instances, after years of saving, slaves had been able to purchase their freedom with these funds.

Johnson, pictured here, may have been smart. Although he would remain a slave for several more years, he would eventually gain his freedom without spending his savings.

WHEN LINCOLN finally made public his plans for the Emancipation Proclamation following the Battle of Antietam in late September 1862, they were met with mixed emotions both at home and abroad.

As a political move, the document accomplished a number of objectives. First of all, it dampened criticism from the Northern abolitionists. Progress was finally being made toward putting an end to slavery.

In the South, it was viewed as confirmation of Lincoln's true motives. His aim was to put an end to a traditional way of life and to sacrifice the rights of individual states on the altar of a strong, centralized federal government.

London's *Punch* saw it as an act of desperation. The Union had suffered repeated losses on the war's battlefields, and the country was growing weary of the prolonged struggle. So here was Lincoln, disheveled (are those horns on his head?), playing the last card in his hand while his gallant and nattily dressed Southern opponent smiles in anticipation of taking the final trick in this game. ("Rouge et noir" was a popular card game of the day.)

The Emancipation Proclamation actually freed no one when it was issued. It said that slaves in the territory then in rebellion against the government in Washington would be free. It made no mention of the slaves in the states still belonging to the Union (Maryland, Delaware, and Kentucky). And since the states in rebellion did not recognize the authority of the government in Washington, they did not feel bound to honor it. Only later in the war, when Federal armies would invade slave-holding territories, would it be used as a legal basis for freeing slaves.

What it did was transform the war from a campaign for a lofty but tangible goal (saving the Union) to a crusade for a noble and righteous cause (ending slavery). In doing so, it blocked any intervention from Great Britain or France. The European powers could not back the Confederacy without appearing to support the institution of slavery.

ABE LINCOLN'S LAST CARD, OR, ROUGE ET NOIR

{ *Punch,* October 18, 1862 }

{V. Blada (Aldabert J. Volck)}

IF LINCOLN HIMSELF was not the devil, at the very least his Emancipation Proclamation was surrounded by diabolical inspiration, according to V. Blada in this privately published and distributed cartoon.

Lincoln is shown working on the document while surrounded by implements of the devil (goats' heads on his chair and worktable; a demon's brew in the cup before him). On the wall above him is a portrait of Saint Osawotamie, a reference to John Brown and his raid on Harpers Ferry, Virginia, an attempt to foment a slave insurrection. In the background is a painting of torture, murder, and rapine taking place in Santo Domingo during the slave rebellion there. And, of course, his foot rests on a copy of the Constitution.

Southerners had a real fear of slave rebellion. Visions of an armed uprising among the slave population of the South had fostered increasingly repressive laws in the opening decades of the nineteenth century. And many in the South now feared that Lincoln's Emancipation Proclamation would spark the violence that was feared most, and at a time when the white male population was away from home and unable to tend to domestic defense.

IT WAS APPARENT late in 1864 that time was running out for the Confederate States of America. Lee and his Army of Northern Virginia had been under siege in Petersburg, Virginia, for months. His army was unable to maneuver, unable to attack, unable to do much of anything other than defend itself. A Federal army under Major General William T. Sherman had sacked Atlanta and was making Georgia howl as he cut a path to the sea. Major General Philip Sheridan was rampaging through the Shenandoah Valley, burning crops, carrying away animals, and destroying everything of value.

The Confederacy was running out of resources and options. There were few men left to fill the ranks. The armies were dressed in rags and were literally starving to death in the trenches. There was but one resource left in abundance—the slaves themselves—and even Lee began to advocate arming the slaves to fight for the life of the Confederate States of America.

At first the Congress sitting in Richmond would not even discuss the possibility. But as the winter months dragged on, even this body began to debate the feasibility.

All this was known in the North, of course. Those newspapers still managing to publish in the South would report on the conditions there, and copies of the papers would make their way north. So the artist for *Harper's Weekly* imagines a chillingly ironic scene where the Southern "Massa" instructs his slave to go and fight for Southern freedom.

STIRRING APPEAL.

CHIVALRIC SOUTHERNER. "Here! you mean, inferior, degraded Chattel, jest kitch holt of one of them 'ere muskits, and *conquer my freedom for me!*"

CHATTEL. "Well, dunno, Massa; guess you'd better not be free: you know, Massa, *slave folks is deal happier than free folks.*"

{ *Harper's Weekly,* December 10, 1864 }

A MAN KNOWS A MAN.

"Give me your hand, Comrade! We have each lost a LEG for the good cause; but, thank GOD, we never lost HEART."

{ *Harper's Weekly*, April 22, 1865 }

FOR ALL PRACTICAL purposes, the war was over when this *Harper's Weekly* cartoon appeared in April 1865. Lee had surrendered what was left of his Army of Northern Virginia. Lincoln was dead. Within days Confederate general Joseph Johnston would surrender his forces to Union general William T. Sherman.

Those who survived would begin to make their way back to homes and families. It was to be expected that veteran would meet veteran while passing on the street or just going about normal course of affairs. Here the artist envisions two such veterans, both amputees, meeting on the street. To the artist's eye, the two have more in common than not.

And while the two might meet and, man-to-man, shake hands in such a situation, it would be a very long time before the two would walk the streets as equals. But, perhaps, a beginning had been made.

· 5 ·

AN OLD STORY, NEWLY APPLIED

The Election of 1864

THE NORTH WAS GROWING weary of war. Almost no one had expected it to last this long. The numbers published by the newspapers of the maimed and of the dead were staggering, and there appeared no end in sight. There was a growing disillusionment with the goals of the war, with Lincoln and his generals, and with the way they administered the chaos.

One strategy of the South was aimed squarely at the general dissatisfaction in the North. By fostering this, the South hoped the Democrats would win the coming presidential election. They knew that if the Democrats won, independence for the South would not be far behind. So the South focused on attempts to undermine the North's willingness to continue, thereby giving Democrats an edge in their attempts to dislodge Lincoln from the White House.

This morning, as for some days past, it seems exceedingly probable that this Administration will not be re-elected. Then it will be my duty to so co-operate with the President elect, as to save the Union between the election and the inauguration; as he will have secured his election on such ground that he cannot possibly save it afterwards.

—Abraham Lincoln,
August 23, 1864

LINCOLN was about to be fired, according to *Punch* magazine. Hunched over his lawyer's desk and chewing on a goose quill, he appears somewhat chagrined as he listens to his client, Mrs. North, give him the news. "We have utterly failed in our course of action," she tells him. She is dressed in mourning garb. "I want peace."

Punch believed it was reflecting the views of the North, and, to a degree, it was correct. Political opposition to the war was growing as the country moved into a year of national election. The victories Union forces had achieved the previous year—Gettysburg, Vicksburg, Chattanooga—were offset by strong negative reactions to the draft, to the new income tax, to rising inflation, and to the lists of casualties. And the war seemed no closer to being won.

The South also wanted Lincoln out of office. It was well understood that for there to be peace, he would accept nothing less than the unqualified restoration of the Union and total abolition of slavery. The South could accept neither point. But, at the same time, it was suffering badly. The blockade was taking its toll, squeezing off munitions and medical supplies, and even such everyday items as needles and coffee had become scarce. The war would not end on terms anywhere near acceptable to the Confederacy as long as Lincoln was in the White House.

Although there were a number of issues before the public—including such items as the admission of new states, the continuation of the income tax, and the like—the only *real* issue was the war: Should it be pursued and the South forced back into the Union, or was it time to pull the armies back and let the South go in peace?

"If you cannot effect an amicable arrangement, I must put the case in other hands," says Mrs. North. It was not an idle threat, and there was a very real possibility that Lincoln would not be reelected.

MRS. NORTH AND HER ATTORNEY

You see, Mr. Lincoln, we have failed utterly in our course of action. I want peace, and so, if you cannot effect an amicable arrangement, I must put the case in other hands."

{ Punch, September 24, 1864 }

THE COPPERHEAD PARTY. — IN FAVOR OF A VIGOROUS PROSECUTION OF PEACE!

{ *Leslie's Illustrated*, July 1864 }

S THE ELECTION of 1864 approached, some of the loudest opposition to the war in general, and Lincoln in particular, came from "Peace Democrats" in the North. Their slogan, "The Constitution as it is, the Union as it was," became a rallying cry for those who opposed the continuing bloodshed. They advocated peace at any price. If the South could be enticed to come back to the Union, it should be welcomed. But if the South continued its demands for independence, it should be allowed to go.

These Democrats were derisively called "Copperheads," a reference to the poisonous snake. But many accepted the name, and actually fashioned lapel pins from copper pennies.

Political leaders in the South encouraged the Copperheads. It was now apparent, to Southerners at least, that they could not win the war and gain their independence through military means alone. A political solution was required, and that would come only if the Cop-perheads gained power. They believed that the North's growing dissatisfaction with the war could only help the Confederate cause.

So the Confederacy adopted a new strategy: rather than winning the war, it would attempt to not lose it. The Confederate armies would stall for time, dodging and retreating and not allowing significant Federal battlefield victories. At the same time, the South would undertake a coordinated series of attacks designed to undermine Northern morale and its collective will to continue the war. From Canada, Confederate raiders would be sent into Vermont. New York City would see acts of arson carried out by secret agents against hotels and high-profile buildings. Camps in the North, holding Confederate prisoners, would be attacked by undercover infiltrators from the South in an attempt to release soldiers for still more raids. And the Copperheads would receive covert financial support.

THE DEMOCRATS were still a deeply divided party when they held their 1864 nominating convention in Chicago. Just four years earlier the party had split along geographic lines, with the Northern faction nominating Douglas and the Southern faction nominating Breckinridge. That split, in the view of many, resulted in Lincoln's election. In 1864, there was danger of another split. Radicals on one side demanded immediate peace, with or without a continuing Union, while more moderate voices called for negotiations aimed at appeasing Southern demands and the restoration of the Union. In casting about for a nominee who could successfully challenge Lincoln this time, the party's leaders wanted a candidate who would satisfy both extremes and prevent another split. The leading contender was Major General George McClellan.

McClellan had been replaced as commander of the Army of the Potomac following the Battle of Antietam. He had not resigned his commission; instead, he had remained in the army, but without duty. He was an outspoken critic of Lincoln (whom he referred to as "the original gorilla") and his policies. He was also popular with the army, and it was thought that he could capture the vote of the soldiers in the field. He wanted the nomination, but was hesitant about the Copperheads' call for an immediate peace.

The artist here depicts McClellan with clasped hands, as if he were pleading with Fernando ("Fernandy") Wood. Wood, a rabid Copperhead, was a power in the Democratic Party. A former mayor of New York, he had suggested at one point that the city secede from the Union so it could continue unencumbered trade with the Confederacy.

Wood is threatening another split in the party, repeating the scenario experienced during the 1860 election, if McClellan won't accept the peace platform as nominee. The negotiation takes place in a tailor's shop with a sign in the background offering to help with turncoats (i.e., traitors).

AN OLD STORY NEWLY APPLIED.

FERNANDY WOOD. "Say PEACE! or, by Thunder, I'll split it up the middle!"

{ Harper's Weekly, July 9, 1864 }

MR. LINCOLN. "MIKE, remove the SALMON and bring me a TOD."
MIKE. "The TOD's out; but can't I fitch something else, Sir?"

{ Harper's Weekly, July 16, 1864 *}*

L INCOLN FACED challenges from within his own party. The radical wing, led by Secretary of the Treasury Salmon P. Chase, believed he moved too slowly on emancipation and not fast enough on the war. Working behind the scenes, Chase actively sought to wrest the nomination from Lincoln during the party's upcoming convention in Baltimore. When word of his activities became public, Chase submitted his resignation from Lincoln's cabinet. Much to his surprise, Lincoln accepted it.

The artist in this *Harper's Weekly* cartoon depicts Lincoln as a diner, who is requesting the removal of one fish course ("the SALMON") while ordering another ("the TOD," a pun on cod). The Tod Lincoln wanted was David Tod, former governor of Ohio. Lincoln had offered him the post of secretary of the treasury.

Tod was a moderate Republican who did all within his power to support the Union. He had defended his state against incursions by Confederate raider John Hunt Morgan and had taken steps against Copperheads, having several arrested on charges of treason. But he was not a radical. His position on many issues closely paralleled Lincoln's. The Senate, like Chase, had been calling for much more extreme measures on emancipation and the prosecution of the war. Since Tod's position was much closer to Lincoln's than to the Senate's, he did not think he would be confirmed, so he withdrew his name from consideration.

THE DEMOCRATS nominated Major General George B. McClellan for the office of president of the United States, and Ohio Copperhead congressman George Pendleton for the office of vice president, during their 1864 Chicago convention. McClellan accepted the nomination, welcomed their support, and rejected their platform.

McClellan did not believe that an immediate end to all hostilities was the solution. Rather, he advocated a negotiated settlement, but one that would call for the restoration of the Union. To simply end the war, in his view, would allow the Southern states to form their Confederate States of America.

This *Harper's Weekly* cartoon tries to capture the Democrats' mixed messages. McClellan, in uniform and brandishing a sword, smokes a peace pipe while attempting to ride two animals, Peace and War, at the same time. Pendleton is astride only Peace, but his position is precarious.

McClellan did not resign his commission and remained a major general through most of the campaign. He was following a tradition set earlier when Winfield Scott, running for president in 1852, refused to resign his commission.

The confusion over the Democrat's position would plague the party throughout the campaign. McClellan's disavowal of the platform was seen by much of the electorate as insincere, particularly since much of the party's campaign material promoted the positions held by the most radical of the Copperheads.

Top: George B. McClellan (1826-1885). Candidate for president on the Democratic ticket during the election of 1864. McClellan's disjointed campaign lost handily to Lincoln, gaining only 45 percent of the popular vote.

Bottom: Abraham Lincoln (1809-1865). The sixteenth president of the United States, reelected to office in 1864. Following a first term marked by open and armed rebellion, as well as divisiveness in the North, in his political party, and in his own administration, there was the real possibility that he would not win reelection.

MARVELOUS EQUESTRIAN PERFORMANCE ON TWO ANIMALS

By the celebrated Artist, PROFESSOR GEORGE B. MAC, assisted by the noted Bare-back Rider,
George H. Pendleton, on his Wonderful Disunion Steed, PEACEATANYPRICE.

N.B. The beautiful creature, PEACEATANYPRICE, recently imported from Europe,
was sired by JOHN BULL, and dam'd by AMERICA.

{ *Harper's Weekly,* October 8, 1864 }

{ *Harper's Weekly*, September 17, 1864 }

LINCOLN'S well-known penchant for homespun humor served as the basis of this cartoon. He would often drive his cabinet, particularly Secretary of the Treasury Salmon P. Chase and Secretary of War Edwin Stanton, to distraction by interrupting discussions of issues with his stories. Invariably, he would start a story by saying, "This reminds me of a little joke."

The gag in this cartoon extends in several directions. First of all there is the obvious play on words, for while in command of the Army of the Potomac, McClellan was called "Little Mac" by the men. And Lincoln the politician was aware of the near absurdity of McClellan's position as a serving major general running on a peace platform that he did not endorse.

Still, Lincoln's reelection was an open question. He himself did not expect to win in November. The election was very much about the war, and it was not going well for the Union during the spring and summer months. Progress was being made, but it was far too little and far too slow to change the mood of the country.

T HE HARDEST SHELL that Jefferson Davis, as symbol of the Confederacy, had to endure was the renomination of Abraham Lincoln for president, or so said *Leslie's Illustrated*. It was clear that Lincoln intended to pursue the war and would not negotiate. With Lincoln at the helm, the war would end only when the South had capitulated.

The Republicans met in Baltimore. Lincoln was nominated on the first ballot, but not without opposition. General Ulysses S. Grant, who was not a candidate, received a number of protest votes.

The Republicans saw an opportunity in the vast difference in their platform from that of the Democrats. In an attempt to court the vote of the War Democrats, they changed the name of their party for this election to the National Union Party, and they nominated Andrew Johnson, a Democrat from Tennessee, for vice president.

THE HARDEST SHELL YET.

{ *Leslie's Illustrated*, July 2, 1864 }

I KNEW HIM, HORATIO, A FELLOW OF INFINITE JEST. *** WHERE ARE YOUR GIBES NOW?
—Hamlet, Act IV, Scene I.

{ *Strong's Dime Caricatures*, August 1864 }

THIS BROADSIDE, published in New York during the campaign, supports the McClellan candidacy by drawing upon Shakespeare's *Hamlet*.

McClellan is cast as Hamlet, and he addresses Horatio Seymour, the Democratic governor of New York. The part of Yorick, the court jester and "fellow of infinite jest" (merely a skull in the play), is played by Lincoln.

When the broadside was issued in August 1864, the Democrats appeared to be in the ascendancy. There was a very real possibility of a President McClellan at that point. Lincoln, presumably, would then be off to a political graveyard.

THIS CURRIER & IVES cartoon suggests that Lincoln dreamed of being chased from the White House by the electorate (in the form of Columbia).

Revived here is the Scotch cap that newspaper accounts had incorrectly placed on Lincoln's head during his arrival in Washington for his first inaugural. Lincoln is pictured as saying, "This don't remind me of any joke!!" as McClellan, suitcase in hand, calmly enters the White House.

It was in August, near the time of this publication, that Lincoln wrote a letter predicting his defeat. "It seems exceedingly probable that this Administration will not be re-elected," the letter said. "Then it will be my duty to so co-operate with the President elect, as to save the Union between the election and the inauguration; as he will have secured his election on such ground that he cannot possibly save it afterwards." He sealed the letter without showing it to anyone and asked that each member of his cabinet sign the envelope.

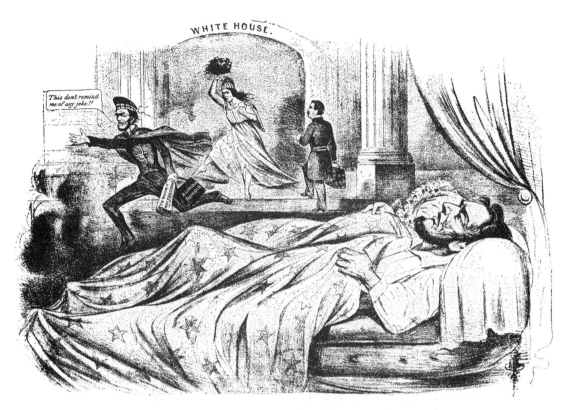

ABRAHAM'S DREAM: "COMING EVENTS CAST THEIR SHADOWS BEFORE"

{ *Currier & Ives, August 1864* }

THE TRUE ISSUE OR "THATS WHATS THE MATTER".

{ Currier & Ives, 1864 }

T HE QUITE LITERAL tug-of-war was obscuring the real issue before the country, according to this broadside published by Currier & Ives during the campaign season. "The Union must be preserved at all hazards!" says McClellan. He stands squarely between Lincoln and Davis, holding them by the collars of their frock coats. Clearly, only McClellan, in the opinion of this artist, can keep the two sides from ripping the country asunder. There is irony in that Little Mac is the biggest man in the contest.

This cartoon started its life in the *New York World* before it was converted for use as a broadside. It is important because it is one of the few pro-McClellan cartoons that received newspaper publication.

Although most prominent Northern newspapers railed against Lincoln because either he was pursuing the war without vigor (the view of the radical Republicans), or he was moving too fast and too far on emancipation (the view of Democrats), nearly all backed Lincoln's bid for reelection.

AS SUMMER became fall in 1864, it was becoming clear that the Chicago platform (that is, the one adopted by Democrats during their Chicago convention) was not the way to go. According to this *Harper's Weekly* cartoon, the way to get to Washington was to take the Baltimore platform (that is, the one adopted by Republicans during their Baltimore convention). The "certain distinguished general" who made the mistake of taking the train from the wrong platform is McClellan.

The fortunes of the Federal armies had turned. Sherman's army had taken Atlanta. Admiral David Farragut had damned the torpedoes and had stormed and taken Mobile Bay. Sheridan had laid waste to Virginia's Shenandoah Valley and driven the rebels before him. The tide of the war had turned from stalemate to Union victory.

In a real sense, Lincoln followed the tradition of the day and never personally campaigned for the presidency. During the election of 1860, he stayed at home in Springfield, Illinois, and let the crowds come to him. During the campaign of 1864, he stayed in the White House and its immediate environs, working on the war. If the country thought the war was going well and should be pushed to its conclusion, Lincoln would be reelected. If the country thought the war was going poorly, and that it was time to pull back and look for peace, McClellan would be elected.

In the end, it made little difference what else happened to be in either the Chicago or the Baltimore platforms. It made little difference what politicians said. The progress of the war would drive the elections.

ON THE WRONG TRACK

A CERTAIN DISTINGUISHED GENERAL. "Say! When does his train start for Washington?"

CONDUCTOR. "Law! If you want to go to Washington, you ought to have taken
the Baltimore Train, which starts from the other Platform. Didn't you know the
Chicago Train don't run to Washington?"

{ *Harper's Weekly*, October 29, 1864 }

{ *Harper's Weekly*, September 3, 1864 }

THOMAS NAST'S most famous cartoon of the war neatly summed up the essential question of the election. Compromise with the South, he suggests, would mean that all the pain and suffering and sacrifice had been in vain. All the battles, all the deaths, had been useless. In the end, the slave owner would prevail. Voting for a Democrat, according to Nast, was the equivalent of a compromise with the South.

There is nothing subtle about Nast or the symbols he chooses to get his point across. In the upper left corner, the Federal battle flag flies upside down (a sign for distress). Columbia, kneeling at the feet of the Confederacy, weeps over Union dead "who fell in a useless war," while a veteran-amputee weakly shakes the hand of the victor.

And the victor is shown to be young, handsome, and strong. He carries a whip in his hand; this he will presumably use on the slaves in the background. In the upper right-hand corner, the Stars and Bars flies proudly. It is emblazoned with treason and slavery and all manner of barbarities.

This cartoon was immediately recognized, upon its publication, as a masterpiece of campaign rhetoric. It was reprinted a number of times and distributed widely during the waning days of the campaign.

LINCOLN WON reelection in a landslide. For the first time since 1836, the country thought enough of its president to give him more than one term.

Lincoln captured 55 percent of the popular vote and carried all but three states: New Jersey, Kentucky, and Delaware. In the army, where it had been expected that McClellan would be strong, Lincoln actually took nearly 80 percent of the vote.

The country wanted the war completed, but it wanted completion on Lincoln's terms: restoration of the Union and abolition of slavery. It wanted Lincoln to finish the job.

LONG ABRAHAM LINCOLN A LITTLE LONGER.

{ *Harper's Weekly*, November 26, 1864 }

L INCOLN WAS NOW a phoenix, according to *Punch*. The mythological bird would die in a burst of flame, only to be reborn of its own ashes. At the hands of the artist, the phoenix became an apt analogy for Lincoln.

The flames arose from the death of such things as the United States Constitution, a free press, states' rights, habeas corpus, commerce, and credit. Once the flames had burned themselves out, Lincoln as this new phoenix would spring to life.

Punch had never been a supporter of Lincoln or his policies, and the periodical seemed genuinely disappointed by his reelection. By this cartoon, the magazine expressed the opinion that with his mandate Lincoln might take on the powers of a dictator, especially since the restraints on his power had been destroyed.

The Federal Phoenix

{ *Punch*, December 3, 1864 }

· 6 ·

A MORE PERFECT UNION?

The Divisive Issues Resolved

WITH LINCOLN CONFIRMED in office and Grant in command of all Union forces, it would be only a matter of time before the Confederacy would succumb to the weight of the North's clear superiority in men and industrial might. At that point, the Union would be restored and Lincoln would finally become president of the United States in deed, as well as in name.

But there were many battles yet to be fought and many men yet to die before the tempest passed. Northern victories came with increasing frequency.

And rumors of peace offerings were given credence by the comings and goings of delegations from both Washington and Richmond.

There was finally some hope that the end of this horrible failure of reasonable men was drawing near, and that the ideals expressed by the Preamble to the Constitution could finally be realized.

We, the people of the United States, in order to form a more perfect union, establish justice, insure domestic tranquility, provide for the common defence, promote the general welfare, and secure the blessings of liberty to ourselves and our posterity, do ordain and establish this Constitution for the United States of America.

—Preamble to the Constitution of the United States of America

THE ARMY of the Potomac was on the move during the early summer months of 1864. General Grant believed his job was straightforward: he was to end the war on terms dictated by the North. In order to do so, he needed to destroy the armies of the Confederacy, the most formidable of which was General Robert E. Lee's Army of Northern Virginia. Grant went right to work, attacking Lee head-on.

"I propose to fight it out on this line if it takes all summer," he wrote to his superiors.

And he did. The Army of the Potomac would smash into the Army of Northern Virginia repeatedly during the summer months. After each battle, Grant would move the army south and east until the armies met again. Lee was forced to follow Grant's moves, staying close and protecting Richmond.

As the Army of the Potomac moved south and east, Lee's army would pivot on its right flank and rush south, attempting to keep up with Grant. While the *Harper's Weekly* artist shows his Northern bias by picturing Lee taking a beating, it was the North that was bearing the brunt of this brutal warfare. Northern casualty figures were nearly twice those suffered by the Confederacy. Still, Grant would not relent.

GRANT TURNING LEE'S FLANK.

{ Harper's Weekly, June II, 1864 }

ABOUT THE SIZE OF IT.

GENERAL GRANT. "Well, and what if it should come to a Kilkenny fight?
I guess our cat has for the longest tail."

{ *Harper's Weekly*, July 25, 1864 }

GRANT WAS WAGING a war of attrition. He had the industrial might and seemingly unlimited manpower of the North behind him, while Lee was running low of both supplies and men. Grant could reinforce his army; Lee could not.

Grant was being called a butcher by many in the Northern press. The carnage was staggering. Critics accused him of waging a Kilkenny cat fight, a reference to an Irish fable about two cats that fought so hard and bitterly that when they were done all that remained were the tails.

But Grant, according to this *Harper's Weekly* cartoon, had the cat with the longer tail.

"I propose to fight it out on this line if it takes all summer," Grant wrote to Secretary of War Edwin Stanton following the Battle of Spotsylvania. The attitude demonstrated a significant departure from former Union commanders. Up to this point, the Army of the Potomac would fall back after doing battle with the Army of Northern Virginia. Grant didn't intend to fall back; he intended to continuously engage his enemy until the matter was resolved.

After Sherman defeated Confederate forces under General John Bell Hood and was able to capture Atlanta in September 1864, he took his army on a march to the sea. With his sixty-two thousand men, he abandoned his lines of supply and communication as he marched from Atlanta to Savannah. Along the way he perfected his form of total warfare by destroying everything of value in his path. It came to be known as his "scorched earth" policy.

Sherman cut a sixty-mile-wide swath of complete destruction through the middle of Georgia. Railroads, bridges, farms, and crops were put to the torch. Livestock was captured; what couldn't be eaten was destroyed. Newspapers reported that Sherman's progress could be followed by the pillars of smoke by day, and the fires reflecting against the sky at night.

He reached Savannah in December and captured the city without a fight. The little Confederate resistance left in that part of the world was simply no match for Federal forces. When he reached Savannah, Sherman captured more than twenty-five thousand bales of cotton and one of the last ports still harboring blockade-runners was finally closed.

"I beg to present you, as a Christmas gift, the city of Savannah," he wired Lincoln. Lincoln gladly accepted.

The artist here pictures Sherman putting the city into Uncle Sam's stocking. It is interesting to note that Sherman is a bit wild-eyed in this cartoon. Following the Battle of Shiloh in 1862, Sherman's pessimism led him to make a number of public statements regarding the Confederates' strength and determination. Local newspapers reported that he was "crazy" and his commanders placed him on temporary leave. When Grant returned him to command, Sherman banned reporters from traveling with his army. He thought them little better than spies and threatened to have them hung. Under pressure from Grant, he later relented. Still, relations were never good between Sherman and the press. Some of this animosity appears to be reflected in this cartoon.

SANTA CLAUS SHERMAN PUTTING SAVANNAH INTO UNCLE SAM'S STOCKING.

{ *Leslie's Illustrated,* January 14, 1865 }

A SELF-APPOINTED ENVOY.

OLD LADY—" *Please Mr. Soger, will you let me take these notions to Richmond. I kind of think they'll convert 'em.*"

GEN. GRANT—" *Guess not! This other is the sort of sugarplum just now.*"

{ *Leslie's Illustrated, February 21, 1865* }

THE SELF-APPOINTED envoy pictured here is Francis P. Blair, who undertook a private mission of peace to the Confederacy in January 1865. The little treats he was bringing to Richmond were his ideas to unite the armies of Lee and Grant and send them to Mexico, where together they would depose the French puppet, Emperor Maximilian, who had conquered the country. Then, while the two great armies were away on that joint mission, authorities of the Confederacy would meet with the government in Washington to effect a reconciliation.

Blair had the connections to make the trip. Retired after a long and distinguished career in government prior to the Civil War, he was well acquainted with the principals in the conflict. Jefferson Davis was an old personal friend. And he knew Lincoln well, too.

One of Blair's sons was a Union general, and the other was postmaster general in Lincoln's administration.

The trip was unofficial, and Blair went without receiving any instructions from Lincoln. Davis warmly welcomed him as an old friend. But since Lincoln had not accepted the premise of two independent countries, the talks went nowhere. No one acquainted with the "notions" expected it to work, but it would do no harm. And it did open a door to the possibility of negotiations.

Blair's mission was a source of amusement in the press. It is lampooned by *Leslie's Illustrated* in this cartoon showing Blair bringing little sweets, but nothing of substance, to his meetings. Grant points to cannonballs as the only treats he's serving at the moment.

Blair's home in Washington, D.C.— on Pennsylvania Avenue directly across the street from the White House—is now federal property. "Blair House," as it is known, is the official guest house for visiting dignitaries.

ALTHOUGH neither Davis nor Lincoln put much stock in Blair's private mission, they recognized it as an opportunity to at least explore talk of peace. With Blair as the go-between, Lincoln and Davis exchanged letters. Populations—North and South—were afraid to raise hopes too high as the parties sat down to talk.

In early February, a peace conference was held at Hampton Roads, Virginia.

In this *Harper's Weekly* sketch of the proceedings, Lincoln is pictured as the big man welcoming the peace commissioners from the Confederacy with open arms. The Southerners are childlike, timid, and a bit ragged.

The South was represented by its vice president, Alexander Stephens; by Senator Robert M. T. Hunter; and by John A. Campbell, assistant secretary of war. Stephens and Lincoln had been friends at one point, when both were members of the House of Representatives. Hunter added stature to the party as a former Speaker of the House. Lincoln and his secretary of state, William Seward, met the delegation aboard a Federal steamship.

The talks went nowhere. Lincoln insisted on a resumption of the Union as a precondition. The Confederates insisted upon separation. After that, there wasn't much left to say.

THE PEACE COMMISSION.

Flying to ABRAHAM'S Bosom.

{ *Harper's Weekly*, February 18, 1865 }

BLESSINGS IN DISGUISE

JEFF DAVIS'S TE DEUM: "Savannah, Charleston and Wilmington are fallen! Our armies
are relieved of outpost duty, and are falling back upon the last ditch! SHERMAN and GRANT are
doomed! Let us await the issue with fitting composure. Allah be praised!"

{ *Harper's Weekly,* March 11, 1865 }

CCORDING TO this *Harper's Weekly* cartoon, the walls were falling in around Davis and the Confederate States of America in the spring of 1865. Davis sits on a teetering, empty keg labeled "Richmond." Around him lies the debris of his house, including the major cities of Georgia, South Carolina, and North Carolina. And bombs are going off all around him. According to the caption, all this is actually a blessing in disguise. Since the cities of Charleston, Savannah, and Wilmington no longer need to be defended, his armies can join and turn with renewed strength to face the armies of Sherman and Grant.

It was a sardonic view of the situation, but it wasn't too far off the mark. The only strategy left to the Confederacy was for Lee and Johnston to combine their forces. Johnston was coming north for that purpose. Lee would attempt one more offensive operation, against Fort Stedman in the Petersburg line, near Richmond. If he could break through, he would lead his army south. Joining Johnston, they would attack Sherman and then turn to face Grant.

Lee's plan worked . . . for about four hours. Lee took the fort, but he could not hold it. At that point in the siege, his army was exhausted and worn out. It was the last offensive operation undertaken by the Army of Northern Virginia.

As the artist indicates, time was running out for the Confederacy.

I N EARLY APRIL 1865, the end of the war was near. The reports that Davis is receiving in this *Harper's Weekly* cartoon are accurate. The Yankees were coming, and there was little anyone could do to stop them. Negotiations had failed. The Army of Northern Virginia was a shadow of itself. Johnston's forces in North Carolina consisted of young boys and old men. The cream of the Confederate fighting machine was gone—either maimed, dead, or taken prisoner. There were very few options left.

There was, however, an alternative to surrender. Davis wanted the armies to simply melt away with their arms and continue to fight a guerrilla war. Johnston by this time had less than fourteen thousand men; Lee about twenty thousand. If only half of these had heeded Davis's call, the war might have continued for years. The Confederate government would move west to Texas, and continue from there.

Grant feared it. Lee refused and did all in his power to quash the idea before it took hold. And Lee's word carried more weight than did Davis's.

Davis made plans to abandon Richmond.

JEFF DAVIS "CALMLY CONTEMPLATING."

"Our country is now environed with perils which it is our duty calmly to contemplate."—
Extract from Davis's last Message.

{ *Harper's Weekly*, April 1, 1865 }

FROM OUR SPECIAL WAR CORRESPONDENT.

"CITY POINT, VA., *April* —, 8.30 A.M.
"All seems well with us."—A. LINCOLN.

{ *Harper's Weekly*, April 15, 1864 }

LINCOLN, as a writer and master public speaker, was rarely given to understatement. Perhaps that is why *Harper's Weekly* chose to highlight this particular dispatch. Lincoln is shown relaxed sitting in his camp chair, using a drumhead as his desktop.

Grant's headquarters during the closing months of the war were located at City Point, Virginia, close to the siege lines at Petersburg. In early April he telegraphed Lincoln to join him, for the final push was about to begin. It was from City Point that Lincoln sent a dispatch back to Washington: "All seems well with us."

This is the most poignant cartoon in this collection. Within days of Lincoln's dispatch pictured here, Lee will have surrendered his army to Grant at Appomattox Court House. The Confederate government will have abandoned Richmond. Lincoln will have visited Richmond and sat at Davis's desk. Understatement, indeed.

And on the night before this cartoon was published, Lincoln attended a play at Ford's Theatre in Washington.

I T SEEMED the world was mourning America's loss. In this cartoon, *Punch,* never a fan of Lincoln, his policies, or his decisions, acknowledges his wisdom and greatness following his assassination. Britannia (symbol of Great Britain) visits Lincoln's bier and places a wreath there, while Columbia weeps at left. At right is a newly freed slave.

Punch published an obituary in verse to accompany this cartoon. In one of those little ironies that seem to populate the history of the Civil War, the obituary was penned by well-known British poet and playwright Tom Taylor. Taylor had also written *Our American Cousin,* the play Lincoln attended that night at Ford's Theatre.

BRITANNIA SYMPATHIZES WITH COLUMBIA.

{ *Punch*, April 1864 }

STOP THIEF!

JEFF DAVIS MAKING TRACKS FOR THE LAST DITCH.

{ *Leslie's Illustrated,* May 20, 1865 }

By LATE May 1865, when *Leslie's Illustrated* published this cartoon, the war was over. Lee and Johnston had surrendered. Lincoln was dead. The soldiers of the Confederacy were making their way back to what was left of their homes. But Jefferson Davis was still at large.

Days before Lee surrendered, Davis and his cabinet had fled Richmond, intending to continue the struggle from other venues. He had been able to elude the Union armies as he made their way south. Along with his cabinet, it was thought, he had the contents of the Treasury of the Confederate States of America. So the artist has now shown him as a thief, running with Confederate gold.

A manhunt was on. The cartoon says that Davis was headed toward Texas, but that was just a guess. It turned out to be accurate, but Davis was taking a roundabout route. He was heading south to Florida, where he hoped to be able to find a ship to take him across the Gulf of Mexico to Texas.

By the time this cartoon was published, Davis had already been captured. He was imprisoned at Fortress Monroe in Virginia while Federal authorities in Washington debated his fate.

THERE ARE AT LEAST two versions of what happened in Irwinville, Georgia, on the evening of May 10, 1865. All accounts agree that Jefferson Davis's party was surrounded and that Davis was taken into custody. This Currier & Ives broadside, *Jeff's Last Shift*, published during the summer of 1865, depicts the event as described in the more derogatory versions.

According to officers present, Davis emerged from his tent wearing a disguise of a woman's overcoat. That account was exaggerated, and soon published reports told of Davis dressed as a woman, complete with hoopskirts and bonnet, and carrying a bucket as if to get water from a nearby creek. According to those same reports, it was his gentleman's boots that gave him away.

When he was finally released from prison two years later, Davis would spend a considerable part of his life writing a history and justification of the Confederate States of America and of the principles his government espoused. And he would spend considerable time attempting to refute the image portrayed by broadsides and cartoons like this one.

Shortly after Davis was captured, Secretary of War Edwin Stanton released photographs of the clothing Davis was reputed to be wearing at the time of his capture. *Harper's Weekly* published this illustration of the clothes Davis wore at the time.

THE CLOTHES IN WHICH DAVIS DISGUISED HIMSELF.

[From a Photograph taken at the War Department by Alexander Gardner.]

JEFF'S LAST SHIFT.

{ Currier & Ives, Summer 1865 }

JEFFIE DAVIS, THE
BELLE OF RICHMOND

{American News Company, 1865}

ALMOST OVERNIGHT, Davis was transformed in the cartoonist's eye from ghoul and devil to clown and buffoon. He was the living personification of secession, the Confederate States of America, and, to Unionists, the absurd notion that the South could survive without the North. Everything about him and his beliefs were held to ridicule.

This five-panel foldout, *Jeffie Davis, the Belle of Richmond,* may be viewed akin to a comic book. Two or three cartoons on each panel recall events during Davis's career as president of the Confederate States of America, all exaggerated and satirical.

Commonly viewed throughout the North as the architect of the war and a traitor to the United States of America, Davis spent two humiliating years as a prisoner in a Fortress Monroe gun casement. His cell was permanently illuminated, depriving him of restful sleep. He was kept in shackles. He was degraded in every possible way, but he was never brought to trial. His treatment finally became an embarrassment, and he was released on parole. His bail was posted by a consortium of prominent Unionists that included Horace Greeley, the abolitionist publisher of the *New York Tribune.*

THE WAR WAS OVER, and Columbia wanted all her children back. This cartoon depicts her waiting anxiously for the return of her "Wayward Sister." In many quarters throughout the North, the seceding states were viewed as "erring brothers" or "wayward sisters." The prevailing view was that they had never really left the Union, because the North had never really let them go.

Now that the war was over, Columbia wanted them to come home. Lincoln's instruction to his field commanders regarding the conquered states was to "Let 'em up easy." There were no trials for treason. Full pardons were granted, usually without question, to those who petitioned the government in Washington. Many former officials of the Confederate States of America, including its vice president, Alexander Stephens, returned to Congress in Washington.

Still, the cartoon is an idealized view. The reality of Reconstruction was somewhat different. Many of the rights promised to the newly freed slaves, for example, would be withheld for yet another century. Occupying Yankee armies were stationed throughout the South to keep the peace and enforce the laws for another twenty years.

THE RETURN HOME.

COLUMBIA. "Tell me, Soldier, did you not pass a Wayward Sister of mine on the road?"

RETURNING SOLDIER. "I did. I fetched her a good part of the way myself, but she says she didn't require my services any more now; and here she comes over the hill."

{ *Harper's Weekly*, May 20, 1865 }

The Publishers

Currier & Ives

Nathaniel Currier and James Ives formed their partnership in 1857. Currier had been active in business for some years prior, but when Ives arrived and demonstrated his artistic and business skills, the partnership was born. They billed themselves as "Publishers of Cheap and Popular Pictures," and during the firm's history more than seventy-five hundred titles were issued. Subjects ranged from domestic scenes and events of the day to politics and historical scenes. During the Civil War, the company issued a number of cartoons generally critical of the South. It built a successful business by providing the public with inexpensive prints. It is estimated that more than a million indi-

vidual prints were shipped from Currier & Ives's offices between 1837 and 1907, when the firm closed its doors.

Frank Leslie's Illustrated Newspaper

Leslie's Illustrated, as it was popularly known, can claim the title of the first illustrated weekly newsmagazine in the country. It was the flagship of the Leslie Publishing Company, which at its peak produced eighty-three distinct publications, including newspapers in English, German, and Yiddish.

Frank Leslie, who launched the publication in 1855, was a talented engraver and businessman. He pioneered the procedures that allowed for the quick production of woodcuts, which, in turn, allowed for the publication of news images within days (rather than months) of an event taking place. The publication was known for its lurid and somewhat sensational reporting and imagery. *Leslie's Illustrated* had a circulation of roughly a hundred thousand at the start of the Civil War, which jumped to well over two

hundred thousand in 1863 before falling again to levels that placed it just behind *Harper's Weekly* as the second-largest weekly publication in the country. The publication took a strong pro-Union position throughout the war, often referring to "our" armies and "their retreats." It continued publication, in various forms, through World War I.

Harper's Weekly
(A Journal of Civilization)

From its editorial offices in New York City, *Harper's Weekly* had a successful press run from 1857 until 1916. Billing itself as *A Journal of Civilization,* it attracted a wide

readership from an audience seeking a sophisticated editorial stance on news and issues of the day. It adopted a pro-Union position during the Civil War. Seeing the success enjoyed by the *Illustrated London News* in England and *Leslie's Illustrated Newspaper* in New York, Fletcher Harper started the magazine as a small (sixteen-page) newspaper. Backed by the considerable resources of the Harper & Brothers publishing house, it was able to attract top-tier reporters and artists. At the outbreak of the Civil War, it had a circulation of 100,000 per week; by the end of the war, the circulation peaked at 125,000. *Harper's Weekly* had no pretense of unbiased reporting and was unequivocal in its support of the Union cause.

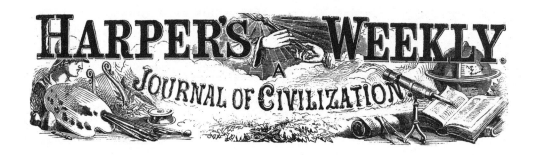

Punch

Punch, the self-proclaimed magazine of humor and satire, was based in London and ran from 1841 until 2004. *Punch* editors boasted of having invented the modern cartoon in 1843 and of having coined the term (see the introduction).

During the American Civil War, *Punch* was a keen observer of political and military events taking place on the other side of the Atlantic. Reflecting the views of the British upper classes, *Punch* took a pro-Confederate/anti-Lincoln stand in nearly all its cartoons, only relenting with the assassination of Lincoln in 1865.

Rail Splitter

The *Rail Splitter* was a weekly publication, as well as a fund-raising vehicle, for the Republican Party. Based in Chicago, it began publishing immediately following the party's convention in 1860, and ran until Election Day in November. It is notable for the series of editorial cartoons that it carried on the front page of each issue. Cartoons of this kind were a novelty on a broadsheet publication of its day, particularly when published at the center of the front page, enough so that the publication had a comparatively wide distribution.

Southern Illustrated News

With the coming of the war, the regular flow of newspapers—including the popular *Harper's Weekly* and *Leslie's Illustrated*—was terminated to the South. A new publication, the *Southern Illustrated News,* attempting to fill the void, was launched in Richmond. It was a weekly, published between September 1862 and March 1865.

The publication was hampered by the availability of materials (newsprint and ink) and craftsmen. Engravers, skilled and otherwise, were rare in the Confederacy during the war years (even the cur-

rency and stamps were engraved in New York). The quality of the product was often poor, particularly in comparison with publications of the North, but it did attempt to present news of the war and home front from a Southern point of view. Its cartoons and illustrations were often copies of those appearing in Northern journals.

Strong's Dime Caricatures

Thomas W. Strong was an artist and engraver working out of offices on Nassau Street in New York City, just a few blocks from Currier & Ives. Strong first came to national prominence in the mid-1840s when he began producing woodcuts for publication in the *New York Herald.* The *Herald,* at the time, was one of the few daily newspapers in the country to carry pictures on its pages. Strong is credited with producing the images of the funeral of Andrew Jackson that constituted the first full page of pictures ever printed in a daily paper.

When the *Herald* discontinued the practice of publishing pictures in lieu of the much more lucrative business of carrying advertisements, Strong continued as an independent artist/engraver.

His output included decorative prints, portraits, and political commentary, and his artwork was in great demand during the presidential elections of 1848, 1852, 1856, and 1860. He was also well known as the publisher of some of the most elaborate valentines of his period. The business did not survive Strong's death in 1866.

Vanity Fair

There have been at least four distinct publications called *Vanity Fair*. The first, a weekly magazine based in New York City and published between 1857 and 1863, had no relationship to other magazines of the same name. The cartoons reprinted in this volume are taken from the first *Vanity Fair*. *Vanity Fair* modeled itself on London's *Punch* (see the representative covers pictured here) and attempted to publish sophisticated articles, humor, and cartoons. It numbered among its contributors some of the largest literary figures of the day. It differed from *Punch* in its attitudes toward the war. In marked contrast to *Punch*, *Vanity Fair* took a strong pro-Union position.

The Artists

FRANK HENRY BELLEW *(1828–1888)*. Born in India, the son of an English mother and an Irish officer serving in the British army, Bellew began his career in London before emigrating to the United States.

His work appeared in *Punch, Harper's Weekly,* and *Leslie's Illustrated,* among other publications. He is, perhaps, best known as the inventor of the character of Uncle Sam. His trademark signature, a small triangle usually appearing in the lower right-hand corner of a cartoon, can be found in a number of the pieces in this volume.

LOUIS MAURER *(1832–1932)*. Born in Germany, Maurer was a student of lithography and mechanical drawing before emigrating to the United States in the early 1850s. Arriving in New York, he secured a position with the firm of T. W. Strong before moving on to Currier & Ives in 1852. During the course of the next eight years, he became the premier political artist of the firm, creating the cartoons and executing the illustrations.

Following the election of 1860, he resigned his full-time position with Currier & Ives to found his own publishing house, Maurer & Heppenheimer. His publishing house was a commercial success, and he was able to retire at the age of fifty-two. He devoted the rest of his life to the creation of fine art.

THOMAS NAST *(1840–1902)*. The German-born Nast was brought to the United States by his parents in 1846. He studied art in New York City until 1855, when, at age fifteen, he brought his portfolio to Frank Leslie and was hired on the spot. He spent three years with *Leslie's Illustrated* before moving on, first to the *New York Illustrated News* and then to *Harper's Weekly*. Shortly before the outbreak of the Civil War he undertook a commission in Europe and spent two years there working for the *Illustrated London News*. Returning to the United States in 1862, he rejoined the staff of *Harper's Weekly*, where he stayed for twenty-five years.

He is credited with refining the symbols of the Republicans (the elephant) and the Democrats (the donkey) and for developing the modern interpretation of Santa Claus in the 1800s, and is often called the "father of the editorial cartoon."

HENRY LOUIS STEPHENS (1824–1882). Born and educated in Philadelphia, Stephens began his professional career in New York City with *Leslie's Illustrated* before moving on as principal artist for the full publication run of *Vanity Fair* from 1859 until 1863.

Stephens was one of the most prolific and sought-after commercial illustrators of his day. His work appeared in a variety of newspapers and periodicals, and he had a successful career as an illustrator of popular books.

SIR JOHN TENNIEL (1820–1914). English-born prolific and highly successful illustrator, Sir John Tenniel was the principal caricaturist for *Punch* magazine from 1850 until his retirement in 1901. He is, perhaps, best known for his illustrations for the original editions of *Alice's Adventures in Wonderland* and *Through the Looking Glass.*

In addition to his work with the *Punch* family of publications, he was known as a serious artist, and his work hangs in London's Victoria and Albert Museum. He was knighted by Queen Victoria in recognition of his work for *Punch*.

DR. ADALBERT J. VOLCK (1828–1912). Born in Bavaria, Volck emigrated to the United States to avoid military service. He lived in St. Louis and in Boston before finally settling in Baltimore, where he attended and graduated from the Baltimore College of Dental Surgery. Dr. Volck then established a successful dentistry practice in that city.

At the onset of the Civil War, Dr. Volck acted on his pro-Confederate sympathies by running medicines through the blockade, acting as a spy and courier for Jefferson Davis, and operating a safe house for Confederate agents passing through Baltimore. He adopted the name V. Blada to give him some anonymity in Union-controlled Baltimore. His cartoons were so acidic in their denunciation of Lincoln and his policies that he ran the danger of arrest. A folio of thirty cartoons was published and distributed during the war years. The publisher's mark carried a London location, but scholars believe it was actually produced, in secret, in Baltimore.

Bibliography

BOOKS

Barnes, Jeremy. *The Pictorial History of the Civil War.* New York: Gallery Books, 1988

Buchanan, Lamont. *A Pictorial History of the Confederacy.* New York: Crown Publishers, Inc., 1951

Caren, Eric C., and Stephan A. Goldman, *The Civil War Depicted in a Display of Rare and Unusual Newspapers.* Brooklandville, MD: Data Trace Media, 2004

Catton, Bruce. *The Civil War.* New York: The Fairfax Press, 1960

Dodd, William E. *Jefferson Davis.* Philadelphia: George W. Jacobs & Company, 1907

Donald, David Herbert. *We Are Lincoln Men: Abraham Lincoln and His Friends.* New York: Simon & Schuster, 2003

Dowdy, Clifford. *Experiment in Rebellion.* Garden City, New York: Doubleday & Company, Inc., 1947

Echer, David J. *The Longest Night: A Military History of the Civil War.* New York: Simon & Schuster, 2001

Furgurson, Ernest B. *Ashes of Glory: Richmond at War.* New York: Alfred A. Knopf, 1996

Gallman, J. Matthew (ed.). *The Civil War Chronicle.* New York: Gramercy Books, 2000

Gibboney, Douglas Lee. *Scandals of the Civil War.* Shippensburg, PA: Burd Street Press, 2005

Goodwin, Doris Kearns. *Team of Rivals.* New York: Simon & Schuster, 2005

Hattaway, Herman & Richard E. Berniger. *Jefferson Davis, Confederate President.* Lawrence, KS: the University Press of Kansas, 2003

Hendrick, Burton. *Statesmen of the Lost Cause.* New York: The Literary Guild of America, 1939

Johnson, Rossiter. *Campfires and Battlefields: A Pictorial Narrative of the Civil War.* New York: The Civil War Press, 1967

Leech, Margaret. *Reveille in Washington; 1860-1865.* New York: Harper & Brothers, 1941

McClure, Alexander K. *Lincoln's Own Yarns and Stories.* Chicago: The John C. Winston Company, 1927

McPherson, James. *Battle Cry of Freedom.* New York: Oxford University Press, 1988

Neely, Mark E., Jr. *The Boundaries of American Political Culture in the Civil War Era.* Chapel Hill, NC: University of North Carolina Press, 2005

Perman, Michael (ed.) *Major Problems in the Civil War and Reconstruction.* Lexington, MA: D.C. Heath and Company, 1991

Pratt, Fletcher. *Civil War in Pictures.* Garden City, NY: Garden City Books, 1955

Reynolds, Donald E. *Editors Make War: Southern Newspapers in the Secession Crisis.* Carbondale, Il: Southern Illinois University Press, 2007.

Shaw, Albert. *Abraham Lincoln: A Cartoon History* (2 volumes). New York: Review of Reviews, 1929

Sideman, Belle Becker & Lillian Friedman, (eds.), *Europe Looks at the Civil War.* New York: The Orion Press, 1960

Wagner, Margaret E., Gallagher, Gary W. & Paul Finkelman, (eds.), *The Library of Congress Civil War Desk Reference.* New York: Simon & Schuster, 2002

Wilson, Rufus Rockwell. *Lincoln in Caricature.* New York: Horizon Press, 1953

MAGAZINES

Bishop, Joseph B. "Early Political Caricature In America." *Century Magazine* 44 (May 1892– October 1892): pp. 219–231.

WEB SITES

Harper's Weekly:
  http://www.harpweek.com/

Library of Congress:
  http://loc.harpweek.com/
  http://memory.loc.gov/ammem/rbpehtml/
   pehome.html

Punch:
  http://www.punch.co.uk/

Son of the South:
  http://www.sonofthesouth.net/

University of Virginia:
  http://xroads.virginia.edu/~cap/
   SCARTOONS/cartoons.html

Image Credits

ARLINGTON COUNTY PUBLIC LIBRARY

Chapter 1—Reads the Papers; "Like Meets Like"; A New Application of the Rarey System; Doctor North to Patient South; Columbia Awake at Last; A Good Boy. Chapter 2—Soon to Be Out of a Job; A "Rail" Western Gentleman; A Job for the New Cabinet Maker; Old Abe; The Flight of Abraham; Our Great Iceberg Melting Away. Chapter 3—All I Want Is to Be Let Alone; Jeff Davis Reaping the Harvest; A "Smash" for Jeff; Capture of Secession Varmints; A Short Blanket; Little Mac's Union Squeeze; Scene, General Head-quarters, Richmond; The Rebel Chivalry; Where Are My 15,000 Sons?; Lincoln's Dreams; The Bad Bird and the Mudsill; The Home of the American Citizen; Mr. Lincoln Finds a Broom; The Naughty Boy Gotham; Scene, Fifth Avenue. Chapter 4—Hello Bill! There Goes the Crisis; A Fish Out of Water; "I'm Sorry to Have to Drop You, Sambo; Rather a Slim Crop; The Rival Cotton Shops; How Jeff Davis Is Saving the South; Who Are the Nigger Worshipers?; One Who Knows His Own Value; Stirring Appeal; A Man Knows a Man. Chapter 5—The Copperhead Party; An Old Story Newly Applied; Mike, Remove the Salmon; This Reminds Me of a Little Joke; The Hardest Shell Yet; On the Wrong Track; Compromise with the South; Long Abraham Lincoln a Little Longer. Chapter 6—Grant Turning Lee's Flank; About the Size of It; Santa Claus Sherman; A Self-Appointed Envoy; The Peace Commission; Blessings in Disguise; Jeff Davis "Calmly Contemplating"; From Our Special War Correspondent; Stop Thief!; The Clothes in Which Davis Disguised Himself; The Return Home. Appendix 1—*Leslie's Illustrated* masthead; *Harper's Weekly* masthead.

KISMET IMAGES

Chapter 1—The United States—a Black Business; The Old Man and His Sons. Chapter 2—Little Stephen A.; The Political Game of Bluff; The Modern Pyramus and Thisbe; The Split-Tail Democracy; President Lincoln's Inaugural; Hab You Seen de Paper Sar? Chapter 3—Up a Tree; "Not Up to Time"; Lincoln's Two Difficulties; One Good Turn Deserves Another. Chapter 4—Shaky; The American Difficulty; Abe Lincoln's Last Card. Chapter 5—Mrs. North and Her Attorney; The Federal Phoenix. Chapter 6—Britannia Sympathizes with Columbia. Appendix 1—*Southern Illustrated News* masthead; Currier & Ives logo; *Punch* masthead.

LIBRARY OF CONGRESS

Introduction—"Join, or Die." Chapter 1—"Miss Columbia Calls Her Unruly School to Order; South Carolina's Ultimatum; Our National Bird. Chapter 2—Dividing the National Map;

The Schoolmaster Abroad at Last. Chapter 3—
Why Don't You Take It?; Jeff Davis Going to
War; The Comedy of Death; Don Quixote and
Sancho Panza; Now, Marshall. . . . Chapter 4—
Under the Veil; Emancipation Proclamation.
Chapter 5—Marvelous Equestrian Performance
on Two Animals; "I Knew Him, Horatio";
Abraham's Dream; The True Issue. Chapter
6—Jeff's Last Shift; Jeffie Davis, the Belle of
Richmond.

MILITARY MUSEUM

Chapter 1—The Fruit of the Palmetto Tree-son;
. . . Or You Are Lost. Chapter 2—The Flag of a
New Confederacy. Chapter 3—Jeff Davis on a
Scouting Expedition.

NATIONAL ARCHIVES AND RECORDS
ADMINISTRATION

Chapter 1——James Buchanan. Chapter 2—John
Bell; John C. Breckinridge; Steven A. Douglas;
Abraham Lincoln. Chapter 3—Jefferson Davis;
Winfield Scott. Chapter 5—George McClellan;
Abraham Lincoln.

SMITHSONIAN INSTITUTION

Appendix 1—*Vanity Fair* masthead; *Rail Splitter*
masthead.

Acknowledgments

One of the best parts of being storytellers, as we like to call ourselves, is visiting the fascinating people who have the stories to tell in the first place. It is the research and the listening to these people that make this job fun. We've met a few during the course of assembling the images contained here.

George Marinos is the founder, the principal curator, and the guy who sweeps up the Military Museum in Gettysburg, Pennsylvania. His is a private museum located adjacent to the battlefield, and it is a treasure. Housed in an unassuming cinder-block building, it contains three floors of perhaps the most amazing privately held collection of military artifacts in the world. No less a treasure is George himself. An avid collector since his high school days, he has assembled literally thousands upon thousands of items dating from the French and Indian War through the present day. He is a wealth of information and most generous with his time. We are very grateful to him for sharing his time, his stories, and his images with us. And we heartily recommend a visit to his museum when in Gettysburg.

This book simply could not have been completed without the assistance of Judith Knudson and her team at the Virginia Room of the Arlington County (Virginia) Public Library. This special section of the library houses a vast collection of information and detail on the Civil War, and the librarians there were most supportive of our efforts. They granted us access to their collections and, at least as important, patience with our fumbling research. We are most grateful to them.

Ellen Nanney, senior brand manager of Smithsonian Business Ventures, gave the initial nod to this work and, working in tandem with Donna Sanzone, our senior editor at Collins Reference, provided continuing support and guidance for the project. It was Lisa Hacken and Stephanie Meyers of the Collins Reference editorial group who labored with the manuscript and wrestled it into a coherent whole. It was their work of prodding writers and crystallizing ideas that gave this book its final structure and flow. We are grateful to them.

These people did their best to keep us on track. Any errors, therefore, belong to the authors alone.

Index

Note: Page numbers of illustrations are in *italics.*